Published by
EN Productions
P.O. Box 1653, Franklin, TN 37065
www.encountersnetwork.com

GET eSchool and Other Materials

The following *Angelic Encounters Today* study guide is great for individual study in your own home, with a small group, or in a classroom setting. It also serves as part of the core curriculum for a course by the same title in our **God Encounters Training – eSchool of the Heart**, which also includes a corresponding MP3, CD and/or DVD class set and other related books. Visit www.GETeSchool.com for more information about this and many other life-changing courses.

At the end of each detailed lesson are simple questions for your reflection and review. In a back section of this study guide, you will find the answers to these questions to aid in your learning.

If you have benefited from this study guide, James W. Goll has many other study guides and materials available for purchase. The companion book to this guide, *Angelic Encounters: Engaging Help from Heaven,* is available from the Encounters Network online bookstore.

You may place orders for materials from Encounters Network's online bookstore on the website at www.encountersnetwork.com or by calling 1-877-200-1604. You may also mail your orders to P.O. Box 470470, Tulsa, OK, 74147-0470. For more information, visit the website or send an e-mail to info@encountersnetwork.com.

Dedication

On behalf of my departed dear wife, Michal Ann Goll, I would like to dedicate this study guide and the corresponding book to both of our devoted mothers who marked our lives with prayer and consecration to the Lord Jesus Christ. Both of our mothers have been a part of the great cloud of witnesses now for some time and have now been joined by the only woman I ever loved.

I love and miss each of you! May your collective prayers continue to fill heaven's bowls and be poured out upon us who remain until that great day when we are all rejoined before the throne of the Almighty declaring together, *"Worthy is the Lamb. Indeed, He alone is worthy!"*

Amanda Elizabeth (Burns) Goll – Mother of James W. Goll

Dorris Grace (McCoy) Willard – Mother of Michal Ann Goll

You shaped our lives to release the fragrance of Christ!

With a Grateful Heart,

James W. Goll and on behalf of Michal Ann (Willard) Goll

Acknowledgements

Every study guide and book I compose is like having another child. A lot of love and nurture go into each birthing. Midwives also help deliver the goods and in this project I have a few that I would like to acknowledge.

This manual is very special to me as it contains the last materials my late wife, Michal Ann Goll, taught. When she was in the midst of the battle for life, we taught this series together. In weakness, she came in faith on two nights of the class, and shared from the depth of her many encounters. So this study guide and the corresponding book are all the more special to me and I trust will be to you.

I want to thank the Lord for the sacrificial service from the staff and extended team efforts of Encounters Network. You have held up my hands in a constant and consistent manner. I could not do carry on with my labors of equipping apart from you!

Your labors of love are noticed and I give thanks to the Lord for each and every one of you who are all known before the throne of God! May our Father in Heaven reward you with many blessings! Thanks to each one of you!

Dr. James W. Goll
Encounters Network
God Encounters Training – E-School of the Heart

Table of Contents

Preface: We Are Not Alone!

I remember so clearly several years ago when I was given a dream from the Lord where I was sitting with various leaders at a "round table" discussion. The question arose, "Who would do a study on angels and their ministry and function today?" Everyone looked at each another and all seemed to indicate that it was not their assignment. In the dream, I was the last to speak. I sheepishly raised my hand and stated, "I will do it!"

So off I went and I studied through the 300 scriptures in the Bible on angels. This was the early 1990s. When I dove into this subject, I realized that when I had pastored in the 1980s I had done a similar personal study at that time. So this was now going to be my second time researching this subject. I read the scriptures; I read all the major books that were written at the time; I did interviews with people who had experiences angelic encounters; and I sought the Lord in prayer.

Little did I know that this was all Holy Ghost prep work as a few months later on the following Day of Atonement our home was invaded with His amazing angelic presence. Oh my! Indeed those nine weeks of visitation changed Michal Ann's and my life forever.

Then, another decade later, I felt directed to study this subject all over again. I got out my Bible and concordance and read the familiar passages. But this time I widened my lens a bit more and gleaned from some of the newer materials that had come out in recent years. Oh what treasures I found! Oh what desire stirred within my being! For the third time in thirty years, I gave myself to study to show myself approved.

I want to experience His supernatural ways! That's what this study guide, the corresponding book and the GET eSchool class set are all about. Want to see, feel, hear and know the angelic dimensions? Do you want heaven to come down to earth? Then study right along with me. These materials have been prepared for those who hunger and thirst to know their Lord in a more intimate manner! Come along with me and together we will grow in grace and truth!

James W. Goll

Lesson One:
Jacob's Ladder Keeps Coming Down

I. IT HAPPENED BEFORE – IT CAN HAPPEN AGAIN!

A. Opening Thoughts from the Life of Jacob

Who could have imagined? Heaven opening up? Angelic messengers coming down for an earthly visit? Promises spoken and revealed. Consider the life of Jacob.

Jacob was destined to be the father of the twelve great tribes of Israel. This young man definitely began with serious character flaws as he conspired with his mother, cheated his older brother, and even deceived his ailing father. Now we find him on the run – like a fugitive fleeing from home, from the God of his fathers, and from his own true calling, destiny and identity.

On the run from Beersheba to Haran, twelve miles north of Jerusalem, Jacob stopped over for a night. There he found a hard rock for a pillow and seemingly sank quickly into a deep sleep. Imagine the scene – by the grace of God, he began to dream. Now going to sleep in that disturbed condition, what he might have received was a nightmarish dream full of guilty and anxious emotions. Yes, the kind of dream from which you wake up exhausted and filled with dread and fear. God would even have been just to have given Jacob a message in this dream full of stern admonitions on honesty and truthfulness warning him of the certain penalty due to the enormity of his sins.

Instead, a gracious God gave Jacob a glimpse of heaven coming down to earth. Heaven indeed opened for this former deceiver, and a ladder with God's own brilliant illumination stretched forth from heaven to earth and back again. And there were angels! Yes, angels without number ascending and descending as God stood at the top of the ladder, smiled and looked on.

Have you ever beheld the beauty realm of God that caught your breath away or brought tears to your eyes? By grace and calling, Jacob beheld the transcendent beauty of God. And he experienced the angels of heaven in an earthly dimension.

Ponder, reflect, muse with me... If God, who is the same yesterday, today and forever, showed Himself approachable and available in the life of Jacob, don't you think this faithful God will reveal Himself to His people today? What happened before – can happen again!

B.   **Gen 28:10-17 – Scriptures from the Life of Jacob**

Then Jacob departed from Beersheba and went toward Haran. He came to a certain place and spent the night there, because the sun had set; and he took one of the stones of the place and put it under his head, and lay down in that place. He had a dream, and behold, a ladder was set on the earth with its top reaching to heaven; and behold, the angels of God were ascending and descending on it. And behold, the LORD stood above it and said, "I am the LORD, the God of your father Abraham and the God of Isaac; the land on which you lie, I will give it to you and to your descendants. "Your descendants will also be like the dust of the earth, and you will spread out to the west and to the east and to the north and to the south; and in you and in your descendants shall all the families of the earth be blessed." Behold, I am with you and will keep you wherever you go, and will bring you back to this land; for I will not leave you until I have done what I have promised you." Then Jacob awoke from his sleep and said, "Surely the LORD is in this place, and I did not know it." He was afraid and said, "How awesome is this place! This is none other than the house of God, and this is the gate of heaven."

C.   **From Matthew Henry's Commentary**[1]

Angels are employed as ministering spirits, to serve all the purposes and designs of Providence, and the wisdom of God is at the upper end of the ladder, directing all the motions of second causes to the glory of the first Cause. The angels are active spirits, continually ascending and descending; they rest not, day or night, from service, according to the posts assigned them. They ascend, to give account of what they have done, and to receive orders; and then descend, to execute the orders they have received. Thus we should always abound in the work of the Lord, that we may do it as the angels do it, Ps 103:20-21. This vision gave very seasonable comfort to Jacob, letting him know that he had both a good guide and a good guard, in his going out and coming in, that, though he was made to wander from his father's house, yet still he was the care of a kind Providence, and the charge of the holy angels. Jacob was now the type and representative of the whole church, with the guardianship of which the angels are entrusted.

1.   God's manifestations of Himself to His people carry their own evidence along with them. God can give undeniable demonstrations of His presence, such as give abundant satisfaction to the souls of the faithful that God is with them of a truth, satisfaction not communicable to others, but convincing to themselves.

2. We sometimes meet with God where we little thought of meeting with Him. He is where we did not think He had been, is found where we asked not for him. No place excludes divine visits (Gen 16:13, here also); wherever we are, in the city or in the desert, in the house or in the field, in the shop or in the street, we may keep up our intercourse with Heaven if it be not our own fault.

3. Note: The more we see of God the more cause we see for holy trembling and blushing before Him. Those to whom God is pleased to manifest Himself are thereby laid and kept very low in their own eyes, and see cause to fear even the Lord and his goodness, Hos 3:5. He said, *"The appearance of God in this place is never to be thought of, but with a holy awe and reverence. I shall have a respect for this place, and remember it by this token, as long as I live:"* not that he thought the place itself any nearer the divine visions than other places; but what He saw there at this time was, as it were, the house of God, the residence of the divine Majesty, and the gate of heaven, that is, the general rendezvous of the inhabitants of the upper world, as the meetings of a city were in their gates; or the angels ascending and descending were like travelers passing and re-passing through the gates of a city.

Yes, what God has done before, He does again!

And the ladder keeps coming down!

II. OUR SON JUSTIN AND THE ANGELS

In February, 1991, at the age of seven years old, Justin Goll, our oldest son received a heavenly visitation. As clouds enveloped his room, and four unusual creatures surrounded the throne of heaven, a ladder descended in his bedroom as angels with heaven's fire manifested in his room. The last angel left a piece of stationery on Justin's dresser with a special word, for me, his father.

And the ladder keeps coming down.

III. ANGELS VISIT THE ORPHANS IN CHINA

Such occurrences of angelic encounters have happened throughout the pages of past and current Church history in many lands and nations.

H. A. Baker, grandfather of Rolland Baker of Iris Ministries in Mozambique Africa today, reports of a visitation that took place in their missionary journey at an orphanage in Kunming, China.

The children who lived at Adullam Home were mostly boys aged six to about eighteen who had been uneducated and wild, who had learned to survive on the streets. At the Home, they were introduced to the Bible and taught to live in a new way. But that's not all. Heaven came to earth, the children were often transported to the heavenly city to be entertained by angels, and their earthly caretakers were taken by as much delighted surprise as the children were. The children discovered the meaning of the Scripture, *but you have come to Mount Zion, to the heavenly Jerusalem, the city of the living God. You have come to thousands upon thousands of angels in joyful assembly* (Heb. 12:22, NIV).

Baker relates: "These happy angels were not only at the gates, they were everywhere. They were always ready to escort the children wherever they wanted to go.... Often in these experiences with the angels our children were given harps and taught to play them and sing as the angels did. They were also taught how to blow the trumpets, as well as much more about the music and language of heaven."[2]

As the Bakers watched, the children, who were swept up into the angelic realm, acted out with their bodies what they were experiencing with their spirits in heaven. The following testimony is an excerpt from the classic book *Visions beyond the Veil.*

"When we saw the children, with closed eyes, all dancing around the room in rhythm, we discovered that in their vision they were dancing with the angels in heaven and keeping time with the heavenly music. When we saw them apparently blowing a trumpet or going through the motions of playing a harp, we found that in the vision they were joining the heavenly orchestra praising the King. We could not see the heavenly harps or trumpets; we could not see the angels' joyful dance or hear their song; we could only hear the children singing heavenly songs. It was a daily occurrence to find a child, lying comfortably on some pine needles in a corner on his own, going through the motions of playing a harp. Going up to him, we could hear him singing a new song we had never taught him.
"As we got nearer still, we would discover that the words were as strange to us as the tune. The singer was singing in the heavenly choir. His song was the song the angels taught him. The words of the song must have been in the language of angels. Seeing the children singing in this heavenly angelic choir was unforgettable." [3]

And the ladder keeps coming down!

IV. EVALD RUFFY'S EXPERIENCE IN CZECH REPUBLIC[4]

In 1991, Evald was a pastor in the city of Libreac, of what was then named as Czechoslovakia. He had a heart attack while ministering in Sweden. During his recovery in a hospital in Sweden, he was released by the Holy Spirit to a "vacation or visitation to Heaven" for three days. During this time he had experiences where he saw angelic intervention as a result of man's intercession.

While Evald hovered on the edge of eternity, his associate pastor named Peter continued to pray for him. Then on the third day as Peter's tears fell upon Evald's bedridden body, Evald suddenly became aware that his work on earth was not yet complete, and that he needed to return in order to complete the will of God for his life. In a moment, Evald found his spirit soaring through the heavens and then hitting his body in the bed. Evald was instantly healed and the doctors declared it a miracle.

And the ladder keeps on coming down!

V. WE ARE NOT ALONE!

We are not alone. We have a *lot* more angelic company that we realize most of the time. Having just a glimpse of the angelic host shows us that we are not alone. Over the centuries, people have wondered how many angels must exist. Of course, there is no firm answer to this question, any more than there is a firm answer to how many stars are in the sky, how many grains of sand are on the seashores of the world, or even how many human beings have ever existed on planet Earth.

Before the throne of God, the prophet Daniel saw *thousands upon thousands attended him; ten thousand times ten thousand stood before him* (Dan. 7:10, NIV). That's not a definite number. It's just a wild estimation of the myriads and multitudes of angels Daniel saw in his vision. Isaiah saw seraphs around the throne (Isaiah 6:1-3). The apostle John looked and heard the voice of many angels, numbering *thousands upon thousands, and ten thousand times ten thousand. They encircled the throne and the living creatures and the elders* (Rev. 5:11, NIV).

You will find angels at work throughout both the Old and New Testaments; more than three hundred times, angels are mentioned or referenced. They are everywhere, uncountable myriads of them.

We are not alone. When we pray, *Thy Kingdom come, Thy will be done on earth as it is in heaven*, we are welcoming heaven's hosts to come and join us, aid us, strengthen us. They're ready to come.

So we pray, *"Lord, we welcome Your angels, Your messengers. We welcome them however they may come. We need help from heaven. We call forth once again for Jacob's ladder to come down to our earth realm, in the Name of Jesus. Amen."*

Reflection Questions
Lesson One: Jacob's Ladder Keeps Coming Down

Answers to these questions can be found in the back of the study guide.

Fill in the Blank

1. What God has done _____ He will do _____.

2. Angels are employed as ministering _____, to serve all the purposes and _____ of Providence.

3. Angelic encounters have happened throughout the pages of _____ and _____ Church history in many _____.

Multiple Choice – Choose the best answer from the list below:

A.	Daniel	C.	300
B.	Isaiah	D.	100

4. _____ saw that "thousands upon thousands attended Him; ten thousand times ten thousand stood before Him."

5. You will find angels at work throughout both the Old and New Testaments; more than _____ times, angels are mentioned or referenced.

True or False

6. Jacob was chosen to be the father of the 12 tribes of Israel because he demonstrated strong character growing up. _____

7. If God showed Himself approachable and available in the life of Jacob, He will reveal Himself to His people today. _____

8. We have a *lot* more angelic company that we realize most of the time. _____

Continued on the next page.

Scripture Memorization

9. Write out and memorize Hebrews 12:22.

10. What was the primary point you learned from this lesson?

Lesson Two:
My Personal Angelic Encounters

The following are accounts of some of my personal angelic encounters.

I. "IT'S TIME TO BEGIN!"

In early 1994, a move of God broke out, and it's still breaking out in the Body of Christ. It goes by various names: "The Renewal," "The Refreshing," "The Father's Blessing," and more. It involves the presence of God manifested in ways that people had never before experienced on such a scale. All over the world, God began to show up when groups of people were worshipping Him in the Spirit, releasing signs and wonders and all sorts of amazing experiences.

In the springtime of that same year, I was in Indianapolis, Indiana, ministering at a gathering called, "City of Destiny." While I was there, I was sleeping in a second-floor bedroom of a house. Suddenly, I was awakened by the sound of a trumpet, although it was more of a shofar sound, and by the voice of the Lord coming through an angel.

I sat up in bed, wide awake. The room was thick with the manifest presence of God. The very atmosphere conveyed the sense of *destiny*. (When angels cross over from the eternal realm to the temporal one and bring with them the manifest presence of God, there can be different "flavors" to the way the presence feels. This time, God's presence felt like destiny.) This sense of God's presence and this sense of destiny lasted for maybe twenty minutes, while I just sat there in the bed, not saying a word. Then, at the end of my bed, I saw an angel.

I don't know how tall this angel was, because the angel wasn't in the appearance of a man. This angel looked more like a "typical" angel, if there is such a thing, covered with glowing, feathery, satiny, radiant white garments. Its wings were held to its sides, and they were enormous. I couldn't say a word. I didn't want to say a word. I was speechless because of the incredible radiant presence in the room and the fear of the Lord and the tangible sense of destiny. I don't know what kind of angel this was, but I know it was some kind of a covering angel or covering cherub, maybe even an archangel—some kind that has authority over other angels. I could tell that much by what happened next.

The angel opened up its wings. I don't know how many wings it had: at least two. Then a hand like a man's hand proceeded out from under the wings. In the angel's hand was a green measuring cup, an incredibly green measuring cup. In this cup was fresh oil. And then for the next twenty minutes, I watched this angel dispatch scores of other angels, hundreds, maybe even thousands of them. They were just taking off as fast as they could, released to go out over the whole world. These angels carried bottles of fresh oil, and they carried bottles of new wine. I was amazed.

Over in the corner of the room, I saw a large bottle of oil perhaps 18 inches tall. The bottle was labeled "Crisco." For a split second, I allowed my unspiritual thoughts to rise up and wonder, "Oh, *why* does the prophetic always have to be so parabolic?" Then, immediately, I understood the meaning. "Oh, of course! It's Crisco. Cris – Jesus Christ." The Greek word is *Christos,* which means The Anointed One. "And the "co" – "the anointing is not being released for one person, but for a *company.*" I understood it – fresh oil was being released through the messengers of Jesus Christ to the company of the Body of Christ.

As these angels were going out, *swoosh, swoosh,* all over the earth, I understood the word that had been spoken aloud at the first sound of the trumpet-shofar. The word I had heard was, "It's time to begin!" It was time to begin a new outpouring. It was time to cross a new threshold in Church history. We had the Jesus movement thirty years before, and now it was time to begin something new.

It's true that something new has been happening in the dozen or so years since then. Something definite did begin then, and angels were (and are) a vital part of it—in response to the Spirit-inspired, fervent prayers of the people of God.

II. AN ANGEL LEADS THE WAY IN MINSK, BELARUS

You may remember the disaster that happened in the nuclear power plant 1986 in Chernobyl, USSR (now Ukraine). The zone of damaging radioactive contamination was still spreading when I traveled to Minsk, Belarus, to serve as a prophetic intercessor for a festival outreach for Jewish people. I had gone there with my two friends, David Fitzpatrick and Richard Glickstein.

After we had pretty much completed our assignment as intercessors for the event, we all felt we had an additional assignment to complete—to intervene in prayer for the protection of the city, especially the children, against what was being called "Chernobyl Disease." It was expected to contaminate the river that runs through Minsk, and if it did, the ramifications for the people would be devastating. We had reconnoitered a bit and we had found a particular place in the city where a bridge crossed the river by some old Communist monuments. We felt that's where we should gather to pray.

So the three of us, who were staying in different rooms on different floors of the hotel, met up late one night to go visit the place we had scouted out during the daytime. We met up on the elevator, and another man happened to join us. When we got out, he got out with us, and he followed us out to the street.

Now, at first we thought we knew where we were going. We had been there in the daylight. But now, not only was it dark, but the subway system, which was immense and complex, was only functioning in a limited way at night. We didn't know how to get to where we thought we were supposed to go. So we just walked down the steps, down to the train tracks. We got on a train that felt to us like the right one. The fourth man got on with us. He looked like a typical Russian man. He said nothing to us.

We got off the train when it stopped, but now we were really lost. We couldn't even remember which side of the tracks to stand on next.

Then the man came up alongside us and he said, in English, "Come, stand over here!" He brought us from one side of the tracks to the other side, where we stood and waited for the next train. When it came, he stopped it, and he said, "Get on here." We looked at each other and decided we didn't know anything better to do, so we got on. That train whisked us away, and when it came to a stop, we got off again. Of course, we still didn't know what to do. Again we crossed over to the other side of the tracks, and again when the next train showed up, the man said, "You get on here!" What else could we do? We got on again, with this Russian-looking man we didn't know, who happened to be able to speak English. (In Minsk, Belarus, there weren't very many people who spoke English!)

We got off again, this time in what looked like a major interchange, with a lot of different exits. We were walking, totally lost. The man got off with us, and he was walking with us. Then he pointed to an exit, and he said to us, "Your assignment rests right out here." We walked up the steps and found ourselves at the exact spot that we were looking for! But now the man wasn't with us. We turned and looked for him. In a split second, I darted back down the stairs to look for him. Of course, I could not find him. He was gone. Surely, our "Russian" guide was an angel.

So we completed our assignment, which involved going down the street to the bridge over the river. We picked up a big tree limb along the way that just "happened" to be there, remembering Jeremiah 23, "the righteous branch." And we took it down to the river to do a prophetic act that was similar to what Moses did in Exodus 15, when he took a stick and put it into the bitter water, and it was made sweet. We threw the branch into the river and we declared that the radiation would not come into this river, that the "bitter water would be made sweet."

Afterwards, we found out that the radiation had never gotten into the city via the river. We had completed our assignment, with the very important help of an angel.

III. WARRIOR ANGELS AND THE BIRTH OF TYLER HAMILTON GOLL

In the middle of the summer of 1988, an important set of prayer gatherings occurred in Evian, France, and in Berlin, Germany. This was before the Berlin wall came down. Instead of being in Europe attending the gatherings, I was at home with Michal Ann and our two young children, because Michal Ann was nine months pregnant with our third child.

Nine and a half months earlier, we had had an extraordinary visitation from three angels. That night, at precisely 2:34 A.M., a wind had blown through the *closed* bedroom window and through our bedroom. It had blown open the bedroom door, gusted down the hallway, turned around, and had come back through the door, slamming it shut. And then it went back out through the same closed window. ("He makes his angels winds..." Heb. 1:7, NIV). Michal Ann and I had been awakened instantly, sitting up in bed together with the wind blowing through our bedroom.

Then, in fast succession, we both had seen and heard and sensed a number of things, some of them together and some of them separately. Michal Ann sensed a broad stretch of angel wings. I heard the voice of the Lord. We both sensed the Holy Spirit hovering over our bed, up by the ceiling.

And then an angel had appeared sort of from the top down, glistening, and the terror of God filled the room. At the end of our bed, there stood a man, dressed in a military uniform—white pants, long red coat, triangular-shaped hat, with a musket by his side. He said nothing; just stared at us. Then he disappeared and another one swooped in and stood in the same spot. This one was also in a military uniform, a dark blue outfit with middle buttons down the coat and a different type of hat. His gun, I remember, had a bayonet on the end. He didn't say anything, either, and then he took off. Shortly after he left, I recognized that these two were messengers or symbols of two wars that occurred on American soil, the Revolutionary War and the Civil War.

Just as suddenly as the other two, a third angel appeared. This one was modern-looking and he was dressed in a modern way—I don't know what branch of the military his uniform represents—and yet it felt futuristic. His presence carried great authority. Inside myself, I thought, "You look like you could be a relative of mine." I somehow knew that, just as the first two represented two wars that had been fought on American soil, this angel could be a messenger of a future war that could be fought on this soil. Then, instead of remaining silent like the others had done, this one spoke. He said, "It's time for Tyler Hamilton." The clock turned to 3:00, and he left. The appearance of the three soldier-angels and some subsequent revelations from God has carried major ramifications, but for the purposes of this chapter, I want to share the part about Tyler.

Fast forward to nine and a half months later. In the wee hours of July 7, Michal Ann was in bed, but I was up praying in our living room. I was thinking about the gatherings in Europe, and I was engaged in acts of identificational repentance because of my Goll (German) ancestral line, confessing generational sins like Daniel did in Daniel 9 and 10, especially repenting for what the Germans had done against the Jewish people and how the Church had not raised her voice during the Holocaust of World War II.

Suddenly, at 1:17 A.M., this same "modern" warrior angel appeared in the doorway of our living room. He said, "It's time for Tyler Hamilton to come forth. You must go and lay hands upon your wife and call him forth."

So I got up and walked into the bedroom. I told my wife, "Tyler's angel has just come." Not that I understood exactly what that meant. I just remembered that nine and a half months earlier, I'd said, "You look like you could be a relative of mine," and I had felt that there was a warrior anointing on our third child. I knew that there are yet many more pages to be written about the wars of the Lord and about our engagement in fighting some of the battles, and I felt that our son would play a role in future spiritual combat.

I told Michal Ann that the angel had told me to lay hands on her and call him forth. She said, "Well, just do it!" So I laid my hands on her protruding stomach and I said, "Tyler Hamilton, this is the voice of your father speaking. Your angel has just come and said that I must lay hands on your mother to call you forth. Listen and obey. This is your father speaking. The time has come. Come forth!" My wife started contractions, and a few hours later on July 7, 1988, Tyler Hamilton was born.

Why did angels have to get involved in this birth? I don't really know. That's the way it always goes. An angelic encounter occurs, often when it is least expected, and it is awesome. I can never comprehend more than a fraction of what's going on; I just try to keep up with whatever God sends my way. Yes, as terrifying as an angelic encounter can sometimes be, I want more of them. Every time it happens, I feel I'm getting another glimpse of our heavenly home, where we'll all be able to see angels all the time.

Reflection Questions
Lesson Two: My Personal Angelic Encounters

Answers to these questions can be found in the back of the study guide.

Fill in the Blank

1. When angels cross over from the eternal realm to the temporal one and bring with them the manifest presence of God, there can be different _____ to the way the presence feels.

True or False

2. Angels always have wings when they appear in the natural realm. _____

3. We may not discover in this life why angels appear when they do. _____

Scripture Memorization

4. Write out and memorize Hebrews 1:14.

Continued on the next page.

Reflection and Journaling

5. Reflect upon past situations where God has intervened in your life. Could angels have been involved? Write down what the Holy Spirit shows you.

6. Write below two main insights you gained from this lesson. Then spend a short time in prayer around those two points, asking the Lord to implant those messages in your heart.

Lesson Three:
Invaded! (Michal Ann Goll)

I. MY STORY

We were living in Missouri, and on a night in October of 1992, there was a great windstorm with thunder and lightning. Jim had arrived home late, after teaching a night class at the Grace Training Center in Kansas City. It happened to be the Day of Atonement, and he knew that often God speaks to His people on that day, so he had led the class in a time of consecration to God, during which the class had felt the supernatural wind of the Spirit and the solemn presence of the Lord in the auditorium. Giving his assistant Chris Berglund a ride home, Jim had commented to him that God was going to come and speak that night.

When Jim arrived home he found our youngest son Tyler, who had been frightened by the storm, sound asleep on the floor next to his side of the bed. He slipped into bed next to me and fell asleep himself.

Suddenly, a lightning bolt struck the back yard, and light burst in through the bedroom window. Jim woke up instantly, but I didn't. A man was standing at the end of our bed! The atmosphere became saturated with the presence of the terror of God, and Jim lay there trembling for one full minute, staring at this man, who was dressed in brown trousers and who was looking right at him.

Exactly as the readout of the digital clock changed to 12:00 o'clock midnight, the angel spoke. He said, "Watch your wife. I'm about to speak to her," and he disappeared. At the same time, the manifest presence of God increased in the room and Jim noticed a supernatural light glowing over our bedroom dresser. I woke up. Jim simply said, "Ann, an angel has just come."

All he had to say was "Ann..." and I was instantly awake. We'd had other experiences with angels visiting us in the night, and immediately I knew that it was about to happen again. Evidently, this encounter was meant for me alone, because—unbelievably—James just rolled over and fell asleep. (We have decided that it must have been a supernatural sleep that the Lord took him into.)

There I lay, on my stomach, with the terror of God thick in the room. I wanted to hide, but all I could do was to wait for something to happen. I gathered all of my courage and I prayed that I'd be brave enough to withstand whatever was about to happen. I really wanted God to come and to give me everything He wanted to impart to me, and I didn't want to interfere with the moment. But I was terrified!

What happened next was surprisingly pleasant. My ears had been hurting for several days. Suddenly I began to feel warm, soothing oil being poured into my left ear. (I was lying on my right ear.) It felt wonderful. Gathering my courage, I turned my head over. The same thing started happening to my right ear. It felt so good. Then more things began to happen.

Pressure started building up in my head. It got stronger and stronger. I didn't know what in the world was going on. Just about when I thought I couldn't take it anymore, the pressure subsided, only to start building against my back. I felt like somebody had placed a board on my back and was pushing me into the bed. It squeezed the breath right out of me, and I thought I must have been making some kind of a loud noise, but Jim didn't wake up, so maybe I didn't. I also felt like the finger of God was working its way into my chest, reworking and rearranging my insides. It was very intense.

Finally, the pushing eased up, and I glanced at the clock again. Exactly thirty minutes had passed. It read "2:04," which later led me to read Proverbs 2:4 [including verse 5]: "If you seek [Wisdom] as for silver and search for skillful and godly Wisdom as for hidden treasures, then you will understand the reverent and worshipful fear of the Lord and find the knowledge of [our omniscient] God" (AMP).

After that, I felt like I was being pulled away from Jim's side while still on the bed. Afraid, I reached out my arm toward him, but somehow I couldn't touch him. Something seemed to be holding my arm back. I don't think my body actually moved, but it *felt* like I was being pulled. The whole thing was really bizarre, to the point that I really began to wonder if it was God.

This series of experiences left me completely undone. I literally did not know if I was still alive or not, and I actually put my fingers up to my neck to see if I had a pulse. I wondered if my hair had turned white or if my face looked different. My skin was kind of cold and clammy. Later, when Jim woke up, he said my lips were purple. The blanket felt real thin. I wanted to hide. I could do nothing to relieve my feeling of absolute vulnerability. I felt so *human* and fleshly. Never before or since have I had such an unnerving experience.

For the rest of the night, I lay there awake. Jim and I would talk a bit, then he'd fall back asleep, then he'd wake up and we'd talk a bit more. We asked the Lord to confirm that this whole thing was from Him by giving dreams to our children. At one point, I was taken up in my spirit for about thirty minutes, and I could look down and see my body in the bed. I saw other things, including a white warhorse, and I heard things. Little did I know that this was just the first night of a long season of these angelic visitations.

The light kept flickering over our dresser (where Jim had left a letter from a seer-prophet that concerned God's call on our lives) until 7:00 o'clock in the morning—I was awake the whole night, absolutely riveted, and basically scared out of my mind. Finally after 7:00 A.M., though, I dropped off to sleep for a while.

Later in the morning when Jim and I woke up again, there was little Tyler standing by Jim's side of the bed like a tin soldier. He said, "Daddy, I just had a dream that an angel came and visited our house last night." His older brother Justin had been sleeping in his bed in the room directly above ours, and he reported that he'd had a dream in which someone took him into a barn to see a white horse—the same white warhorse that I had seen. There was the confirmation we had asked for.

Somehow, there was grace to get through the daylight hours. We were supposed to home school, but no way was it a normal day. I felt like there was a whole encampment of angels in the house. There was such an awesome presence of God's glory throughout every room. Every time I walked into a room, I didn't know what or whom I was going to see. I just walked around feeling a kind of strange expectation. I'd think, "Oh, yeah – I need to fix breakfast for the kids.... Oh, yeah, I need to fix GraceAnn's hair." (I even forgot how to do that at one point.) Once, I was sitting on the couch and GraceAnn, who was five at the time, walked up behind me and touched me. I nearly jumped out of my skin!

I found something in the book of Job that helped me describe this experience:

> *Now a thing was secretly brought to me, and my ear received a whisper of it. In thoughts from the visions of the night, when deep sleep falls on men, fear came upon me and trembling, which made all my bones shake.* Job 4:12-14, (AMP)

I remembered biblical accounts of angelic visitations, for example what happened to the shepherds at Bethlehem the night Jesus was born. There's a *reason* they fell down. There's a reason Daniel fell "like a dead man." There's a reason the angels are always saying, "Fear not." It's a fearful thing when God unzips his Superman suit a little and lets some of His glory shine out. Our mortal bodies just can't handle it, even a small taste.

With the help of a discerning friend, I began to realize that the different aspects of that first night had meaning for the broader Body of Christ. It was as if I had entered into a prophetic intercessory experience that had implications for the Church as a whole. For instance, the intense pressure in my head and the incredible pushing on my back represented God's desire to push fear and unbelief out of His Bride. That's why I felt like my heart had stopped. It was as if Jesus came and said, "I want to rearrange your heart. My own heart cries out for an exclusive relationship with you." That's why I couldn't hold onto Jim in the night; the Lord wanted me to cling to Him alone. The Lord was saying, "I am jealous after you with true jealousy, and I will not be satisfied to have a relationship with you through your husband, your pastor, or anyone else."

After the first night, more angelic visitations occurred. In fact, they occurred, to one degree or another, every night for weeks and weeks. I believe that the main reason the angels came was so that I could be closer to Jesus. I said as much to Him: "Lord, if these experiences don't draw me closer to You and don't reveal more of Yourself to me, then of what use are they?"

The Lord Jesus wants to enable the whole body of believers to have unimpeded communion with Him. He is coming to restore the earth. He's coming to push fear and unbelief out of His Bride, the Church. He's coming to open our ears so that we can hear like a disciple. As I learned, His angelic messengers are not always very quiet and gentle when they help us hear Him.

Everything was different for a while. Instead of settling down for a night's sleep, I would gear up for the angels to come. They would wake me up by slapping my feet or slapping my shoulder. (Remember how the angel woke Peter up when he was in prison? "Suddenly an angel of the Lord appeared and a light shone in the cell. He struck Peter on the side and woke him up"—Acts 12: 7a, NIV.) It was as if they were saying, "Wake up! Wake up! You *can't* be asleep!"

I remember one Saturday morning. Jim was gone. (He had a grueling travel schedule much of that year.) All of a sudden, I became aware that someone had touched me on my left hand with two fingers. It was no normal touch; the instant I was touched, my hand was filled with energy and heat. Liquid fire flowed over to my right hand. It began to spread down to my feet. It coursed all through my body for about 30 minutes. I was just gyrating. Afterward, I turned on the light, and my hands were actually pink and a little swollen—and there was a white spot in the middle of my hand, right where I had been touched. These experiences were *not* comfortable.

Over and over, I would become too scared to handle it. I just felt like I wasn't going to live through it. I'd beg the Lord to ease up. "Oh, Lord, I'm sorry but I'm just going to ask You not to come. Please don't come. This is too intense." Then the next morning, I'd be frustrated with myself that I had been such a scaredy-cat. I'd tell the Lord, "I'm sorry about what I said in the night. I really want You to come. I really do." Then nighttime would come, and I'd get scared all over again. Finally, I thought I had figured out how to pray. I would say, "Lord, I want You to listen to the prayers of my strength. Don't listen to the prayers of my weakness. If tonight I tell you not to come, don't listen to me. I really do want you to come!"

But the Lord didn't want me to pray that way for very long. He simply said, "What do you want? I want to come and visit you. There are things that I want to give you. I promise that I'll never leave you nor forsake you. But if you really don't want me to come like this, then I will stop coming. I want you to stop praying like this. Stop vacillating. Decide once and for all what you really want. Then tell Me."

It took me three days to make up my mind, and I shed lots of tears. This was no small matter. The fear of the Lord is clean, and it's not like the fear of an enemy, but it's terrifying just the same.

Finally, after three days of saying, "God help me," I yielded. I told him I really wanted Him to come, and that I wasn't going to go back and forth anymore. I told Him I meant it, even if it meant I would die in the process. I told Him I had no place else to go for Life, and that I would leave my fears behind.

So He did keep coming.

The angelic visitations would get really intense when Jim was out on the road. When he'd come home, they would be more subdued. I wanted him to have these experiences with me, but it was as if the Lord had reserved them mostly for me.

Every evening at about 9:00 P.M., God's presence would begin to intensify. It seemed to reach a peak by about 11:00 P.M., and then I would be awake until about 4:00 in the morning, night after night. During the day, God would give me grace and He would give the kids grace too. They would be all right when I'd fall asleep during the day. There were people who came in and helped me. It was a season of grace.

No two experiences were alike. The same night I had the liquid fire going through me, I remember dropping off to sleep after a few hours and beginning to dream. In the dream, I was carrying on a conversation with someone I know, and he was telling me something about a changing table (which had become a standard piece of furniture in our household full of small children in diapers). Then he was walking around my room inspecting the heat vents and talking to me about being susceptible to allergies. As the dream progressed, I began to realize that I was *hearing* this person as he walked around, because he had squeaky shoes. Then I began to realize that it was more like my dream was blending with reality, as dreams sometimes do, because I really was hearing somebody's squeaky shoes walking around my bedroom. He'd squeak into the bathroom, back into the room, walking around and talking with me about things. I heard him come around the bed. Finally, I opened my eyes and here was this angel who looked just like the person in the dream. The dream and reality blended together. I felt like I had been having this long conversation with the angel, and that it was the same angel who had touched me on the hand earlier. I felt like I'd been trying to find him in the hours since then. He was transparent, but he had brown hair that came down below his chin. He was wearing glasses and brown clothes. I blurted out, "There you are! Hi! Why are you here?" Instantly, he vanished.

Night after night, strange and wonderful things would happen. Sometimes, I would have sensations such a bitter taste on the tip of my tongue or a burning on my lips. Sometimes, my tongue would get hard or my ears would pop or my nose would open up. I knew that the Lord was telling me there would come a time when I would have "hard faith," when I would have to say bitter things that people might not want to receive.

One night, fireballs showed up by the ceiling. First I became aware of flashes of heat coming down over me, and then I saw a white fireball in the air and it came down and hit me. I said "Oh, Lord, do it again. I want you to come. I want you to come and visit me as much as you want to." I felt that the challenge from the Lord was to engage in what He was doing, to get every last drop out of what He wanted to release to me. Another fireball appeared. It was burning and rotating, like it was set, ready to go. I said, "Hit me! Hit me!" and it just flew toward me and exploded in my chest. Then I'd say, "I want another one! Another one!" And another one would appear up by the ceiling. The fire of God would be released inside of me, and I kept calling for more. As long as they kept showing up, I kept calling for more, until maybe twelve or fifteen of them had been released.

After a while, the Lord gave me a promise. He said, "Next time, not only will the angels come. Now, Jesus Himself will come." That put everything into perspective.

I had been trying to journal everything, to keep track, which I believe the Lord wanted me to do. I wanted to understand it. But it became such a huge mountain of information! So much of it was in riddles. Sometimes I didn't know how to write it down. I had so many questions that were not being answered at the time. I was getting more questions than I was getting answers. It seemed too much for me to process.

I would have dreams where I would hear Jesus singing, "Where is My Bride, oh My God?" He was longing for his Bride to be ready for Him. He hears us sing our worship songs in church. We sing, "Let me feel the kisses of Your mouth. Let me feel your warm embrace," and *Jesus thinks we mean it!* We are arousing His love, but we don't know what we're doing. He's coming in response, and we don't even recognize it. We don't even know what He looks like. His heart is breaking, and He's asking, "Where is My Bride, My God?"

My heart broke as I began to understand. He was shattering the hardness of my heart. He was making me able to hear what His heart was saying, and He was giving me an intercessory burden for the Body of Christ. He was making me able to release His love to His Bride, and to release my love back to Him in prayer.

I didn't want to have experiences for the sake of having experiences. I didn't want to have them just so I could stand up in front of a group of people and say, "I've had angelic encounters." I wanted to have these experiences and to be able to tell about them only for the sake of testifying about His love. I wanted to be able to impart some of His powerful love to others.

My special season of angelic encounters ended after nine weeks. Toward the end, I felt like I could finally understand the Song of Solomon, because my heart was lovesick for the Lord. I knew that the season was changing and I knew that what I had been experiencing was drawing to a close. I did everything I knew how to do to extend it. As frightening as it was, I did not want to have that chapter closed. I was lovesick. My heart was sick with love.

The Lord had allowed me to come into such a precious place in Him. He had shared such deep things with me. I couldn't imagine going back to regular routines, going to bed and sleeping all the way through the night, waking up thinking about what I was going to do that day, doing chores, going shopping for groceries, and cooking dinner. I didn't want to go back to regular life. I was hungry for more of Him.

I came away from this time a changed person. No longer was I intimidated by other people. Now I had a new level of authority, even though I was not really aware of it. Jim said, "I don't know who you are, or who you are becoming." I didn't know who I was either. He was shocked at the waves of authority he could feel when I even waved my hand toward him. The changes in me meant changes in our marriage. We had to make some adjustments.

Jim says he had thought he was married to the perfect wife, because I was totally compliant. And then when I got delivered from my fear of man, fear of rejection, and so forth, I became, in his words, a *lioness*. At first he thought he had liked me better before, when I was real quiet, but then we decided that God was re-making both of us into His image. As we were becoming more like Jesus, we'd have to continue to make more adjustments to each other. The important thing was to champion each other's journey—and to keep growing with Him.

Nine weeks was the equivalent of a nine-month gestation period. It was like a prophetic parable we walked through, because the Lord came to visit a bride (me) and He did things that showed us what He wants to do for his Bride, the Church. Just as the angel spoke to Jim and said, "Watch your wife. I'm about to speak to her," the message that's being spoken to the corporate Church is "Watch my Bride. I'm about to speak to her.

Speak to us, Lord. Let that word come. Let the light shine. Angelic visitors, come and do God's bidding. May the light of His brilliance invade us and draw us into a greater intimacy with the Father, Son, and Holy Spirit, for the sake of Jesus Christ, our Savior. Amen.

Reflection Questions
Lesson Three: Invaded! (Michal Ann Goll)

Answers to these questions can be found in the back of the study guide.

Fill in the Blank

1. There's a good reason why angels said, "_____ _____" to those they visited in the Bible.

2. God is jealous that we have an intimate _____ with Him. He wants us to _____ to Him alone.

3. God comes to open our ears so that we can hear like a _____.

Multiple Choice – Choose the best answer from the list below:

A.	Devotion	C.	Fear
B.	Communion	D.	Encounters

4. The Lord Jesus wants to enable the whole body of believers to have unimpeded _____ with Him.

5. He's coming to push _____ and unbelief out of His Bride, the church.

True or False

6. The main reason the angels came was so that I could be closer to Jesus. _____

7. Angelic messengers are always quiet and gentle when they help us hear Him. _____

Continued on the next page.

Reflection and Journaling

8. Have you ever felt "invaded" by God? Write down how God has taken the initiative to reach out to you and what the result has been. If you have resisted His coming to you, affirm that you want to leave your fears behind and welcome His work in your life.

Lesson Four:
The Nature of These Celestial Beings

I. WHO ARE THESE HEAVENLY BEINGS?

A. From the Protestant Reformer Martin Luther

Martin Luther, in his book *Table Talk,* gave us a wonderful definition of who these celestial beings are: "An angel is a spiritual creature created by God without a body, for the service of Christendom and the church." [5]

B. From the Reformed Theologian John Calvin

John Calvin in his *Institutes* stated, "The angels are the dispensers and administrators of the Divine beneficence toward us; they regard our safety, undertake our defense, direct our ways, and exercise a constant solitude that no evil befall us." [6]

C. From Contemporary Writer Margaret Barker

Margaret Barker in her insightful book *An Extraordinary Gathering of Angels*, remarks, "Angel means messenger, and humans experience angels primarily as messengers. But this is not what they are; this is what they do. Angels exist to praise God, and humans who experience their presence are bring guided toward this universal hymn of praise. Mystics and seers have heard their song, and those who respond to the angels' message move inevitably toward the harmony the angels represent, the "peace on earth" of the Bethlehem angels. By joining the song of the angels, human hearts and minds are connected to the power of the invisible creation, and their lives are renewed." [7]

D. From a Catholic Church Perspective

From another Church history perspective, Father Pascal Parente composed, "The Angels are spirits," says Augustine In his sermon on Psalms 103, "but it is not because they are spirits that they are Angels. They become Angels when they are sent, for the name Angel refers to their office not to their nature. You ask the name of this nature, it is spirit; you ask its office, it is that of an Angel, (i.e., a messenger). In as far as he exists, an Angel is a spirit; in as far as he acts, he is an Angel." The word "angel" comes from a Greek word meaning "messenger." In the Scriptures of the Old Testament, the most frequently used name to designate the Angels is *mal'akh,* which means, messenger or legate." [8]

E. From a Jewish Theological Background

Rabbi Geoffrey W. Dennis gives a peak into the role of Angels in Jewish Tradition, "From ancient times, Jewish tradition has recognized that God's manifold creation includes spiritual as well as material entities. In the Bible, there are a wondrous variety of numinous creatures that serve the God of Israel; *Seraphim* (Fiery Ones), *Cherubim* (Mighty Ones), *Chayyot* (Holy Beasts), *Sarim* (Princes), *Ophanim* (Wheels), and *Melachim* (Messengers). These creatures, collectively known as *B'Nei ha-Elohim* (Divine Beings) and/or *Kedoshim* (holy ones), are assembled into an *Adat El* (divine assembly). Most of these entities are anonymous, but a few have names. Subsequently all these divine beings are subsumed under the term *malach* (messenger/angel). [9]

F. From a Modern Day Evangelical

From the evangelical statesman of our time, Billy Graham, we find, "Angels belong to a uniquely different dimension of creation that we, limited to the natural order, can scarcely comprehend. In this angelic domain the limitations are different from those God has imposed on our natural order. He has given angels higher knowledge, power and mobility than we.... They are God's messengers whose chief business is to carry out His orders in the world. He has given them an ambassadorial charge. He has designated and empowered them as holy deputies to perform works of righteousness." [10]

II. VIEWS CONCERNING ARCHANGELS

A. The Use of the Term Archangel in Scripture

This term is used to denote covering angels with the rank of having other angels under their command. Here are some examples:

1. I Thessalonians 4:16 – *For the Lord Himself will descend from heaven with a shout, with the voice of an archangel, and with the trumpet of God. And the dead in Christ will rise first.*

2. Jude 9 – *Yet Michael the archangel, in contending with the devil, when he disputed about the body of Moses, dared not bring against him a reviling accusation, but said, "The Lord rebuke you!*

3. Ezekiel 28:14 – *You were the anointed cherub who covers; I establish you: You were on the holy mountain of God; You walked back and forth in the midst of fiery stones.*

4. Revelation 12:3, 4 – *And another sign appeared in heaven: behold, a great, fiery red dragon having seven heads and ten horns, and seven diadems on his heads. His tail drew a third of the stars of heaven and threw them to the earth. And the dragon stood before the woman who was ready to give birth, to devour her Child as soon as it was born.* (See also Revelation 12:7-12.)

B. The View of Three Original Archangels

The word *archangel* is actually only specifically used only one time with a name of an angel following and that is in Jude 9 in reference to Michael. Evangelical and charismatic teachings typically refer to there being three original archangels: Lucifer, Gabriel and Michael.

1. Lucifer
    This is the original name for Satan before he fell into sin and rebellion against God.

    a) Isaiah14:12 – *How you are fallen from heaven, O Lucifer, son of the morning! How you are cut down to the ground. You who weakened the nations!*

    b) Ezekiel 28:13, 14 – *You were in Eden, the garden of God; Every precious stone was your covering: The sardius, topaz, and diamond, beryl, onyx, and jasper, sapphire, turquoise, and emerald with gold. The workmanship of your timbrels and pipes was prepared for you on the day you were created. You were the anointed cherub who covers.*

    c) Luke 10:18 – *Jesus said, "I was watching Satan fall from heaven like lightning."*

    d) Revelation 12:3, 4, 7-12 – *And behold, a great red dragon…swept away a third of the stars of heaven and threw them to the earth. And there was war in heaven, Michael and his angels waging war with the dragon. The dragon and his angels waged war, and they were not strong enough, and there was no longer a place found for them in heaven. And the great dragon was thrown down, the serpent of old, who is called the devil and Satan, who deceives the whole world.*

2. Gabriel
    This angel is mentioned five times in scripture – notice the terms "the man Gabriel." Every time Gabriel is mentioned, he brings a specific message and presence of the Lord. Thus, the term Messenger Angel has been coined.

      a)   Daniel 8:16-19 – An audible voice called Gabriel by name to come to the help of Daniel so that he could understand the meaning of a vision.

      b)   Daniel 9:20-27 – Gabriel was *"caused to fly swiftly, touched me."*

      c)   Daniel 10 – God responded to Daniel's intercession immediately by sending the angel Gabriel, but this angel had to fight for twenty-one days and needed the assistance of another angel, Michael, in order to get through to the prophet.

      d)   Luke 1:19 – Gabriel announced himself and his mission to Zecharias.

      e)   Luke 1:26 – Sent to Mary in the city of Nazareth in Galilee.

3.   Michael

Michael is seen to be involved in warfare and arguing with the devil, he has warring angels under his covering, and he is particularly used to defend Israel. Thus, the term Warrior Angel has been used. This angel is mentioned four times in scripture.

      a)   Daniel 10:21 – *"Your prince."*

      b)   Daniel 12:1 – *"Great prince."*

      c)   Jude 9 – Offered no *"railing accusation"* against the devil, but calmly and with great authority and security rebuked him.

      d)   Revelation 12:7-9 – *"Michael and his angels fought against the dragon; and the dragon fought and his angels."*

C.   Other Historical Thoughts on Additional Archangels

Various Christian traditions name other archangels, such as Raphael and Uriel.[11] Some people believe that the angel who came to stir the waters at the pool of Bethesda (see John 5) was the one named Raphael, whose name means "the healing of God." People say he is sent to heal the damage done by demons. We read about Raphael (as well as Uriel, both mentioned in company with Michael and Gabriel) in the Book of Enoch, which is not included in the canon of Scripture, although it is quoted from in the book of Jude (see Jude 1:14).[12] Raphael is one of the principal characters in the deuterocanonical book of Tobit, and in Jewish tradition Uriel, whose name means "fire of God," is the cherub with the fiery sword who barred the gate to Eden.

1.   Catholic View of Three Current Ruling Archangels:
Michael, Raphael, and Gabriel

2.   Enoch and the Four Archangels
Michael, Uriel, Raphael, and Gabriel

3. Other Thoughts – The Nine Choirs of Angels
    A traditional hierarchy of angels ranked from lowest to highest into the following nine orders: angels, archangels, principalities, powers, virtues, dominions, thrones, cherubim, and seraphim.[13]

III. THE ESSENCE OF ANGELS

A. Language Forms

1. I Corinthians 13:1 – Possible language form unknown to man.
2. Speak in dialects known to man.
3. Scripture indicates that angels both speak softly and shout.
4. Sing praises to God and before man.

B. Wings
Some angels have two, four, or six wings.

C. Garments

1. Matthew 28:2-4 – Garments as white as snow.
2. Acts 1:9-11 – Two angels appear as men in white clothing.

D. Lightning

1. Luke 10:18 – Jesus commenting on His pre-existence in heaven, said that He *"beheld Satan as lightning fall from heaven."*
2. Ezekiel 1:4, 7, 14 – *A fire enfolding itself... brightness was round about it... they sparkled like the color of burnished brass... the living creatures ran... as the appearance of a flash of lightning.* (KJV)

E. Instruments

1. I Thessalonians 4:16 – Trumpet.
2. Revelation 8:2, 6 – Seven angels and seven trumpets. (Particularly when announcing God's will, in preparation of coming judgment.)

F. Appearance as Men

1. Genesis 19:1, 5, 8, 10 – There are numerous accounts of this.
2. Hebrews 13:2 – We need to remember hospitality to strangers because some have thus entertained angels unawares.
3. Angels may look, talk, act like, and dress like normal people from various cultures and ethnic origins.

G. Winds and Fire

1. Hebrews 1:7 – *Of the angels He [God] saith, "Who maketh his angels spirits, and his ministers a flame of fire."* (KJV)
2. Psalms 104:4 – This is the Old Testament text that the writer of Hebrews is quoting above.

IV. CONCLUSION

Sometimes it seems to me that the invisible veil that separates the heavenly (eternal) realm from the earthly (temporal) realm is becoming thinner all the time, especially when you hear testimonies like the ones I quoted in the first chapter from H.A. Baker's book, Visions Beyond the Veil. There seems to be more visiting going back and forth between the two realms than we realize.

We know that the heavenly realm will never pass away, whereas the earthly realm will, at some point, be devoured by fire. That's why the planet Earth is called "temporal"; it's temporary. Where does this temporal world end and eternity begin? You can't tell, because so much of the Kingdom of God is here now. We don't have to wait until we die to experience it. It's here already. That's what Jesus had in mind when he taught us to pray, *"Thy kingdom come, thy will be done, on earth as it is in heaven"* (Luke 11:2, KJV). When we pray that prayer, we are asking God, as His children, to send reinforcements.

In heaven, they are waiting to come to our aid, and they pass over easily from the eternal to the temporal realm. We may not see them, but that doesn't mean they haven't come. (Or we may actually see them or sense their nearness, but that doesn't mean we're crazy!)

Reflection Questions
Lesson Four: The Nature of These Celestial Beings

Answers to these questions can be found in the back of the study guide.

Fill in the Blank

1. The word "angel" comes from a Greek word meaning "_____."

2. God has designated and empowered angels as holy _____ to perform works of _____.

3. List five names of angels that various traditions consider archangels:

   a. _____   d. _____

   b. _____   e. _____

   c. _____

Multiple Choice – Choose the best answer from the list below:

A.	New	C.	Symbols
B.	White	D.	Dialects

4. Angels can speak in _____ known to man.

5. The Bible describes angels appearing in _____ clothing.

True or False

6. Angels have different rank. _____

7. Some angels have two, four, or six wings. _____

8. Angels may look, talk, act like, and dress like normal people from various cultures and ethnic origins. _____

Continued on the next page

Scripture Memorization

9. Write out and memorize Hebrews 13:2.

10. Write below two main insights you learned about the nature of angels.

Lesson Five:
The Characteristics of Angels

I. MORE ANGELS AMONG US!

A. How Many Are With Us?

1. From Thomas Aquinas
   Thomas Aquinas, an early Church theologian and logician, believed there are many times more angels than there were human beings.

2. From Charles Ryrie
   Theologian Charles Ryrie says that some have suggested there are as many angels in the universe as the total number of all human beings throughout history.

3. From Clement of Alexandria
   Clement of Alexandria in the second century A. D. suggested that there are as many angels as there are stars in the stellar heavens. This line of thinking is based on the idea that angels as associated with the stars in scripture (Job 38:7; Psalm 148:1-3; Revelation 9:1-2; 12:3-4, 7-9).

   If Clement is correct, the number of angels would exceed the stars visible to the human eye-approximately 6,000 during the year. Scientists say the total number my run into the billions!

4. Some Additional Thoughts
   The number of angels is vast indeed. Luke 2:13 tells us that we are surrounded by "a great company of the heavenly host." Psalm 68:17 and Daniel 7:10 state that there are "ten thousands of thousands." From that count we come up with 100,000,000 (100 million). Revelation 5:11 describes the number as "myriads of myriads." I agree with Job 25:3 where it recites for us, *"Can his forces be numbered?"*

   Scripture never clearly specifies for us just how many angels there are. Angels do not die, nor do they propagate and give birth to baby angels. The number of angels remains constant since the fall.

B. Various Titles Given in Scripture

1. Angels referred to as Sons of God
    Job 1:6, 2:1, 38:7 (KJV)
    In this case son(s) of is a reference to being "of the order of" or "in the order of God" not that the angels are literally sons of God – Jesus Christ is the only Son of God.

2. Angels referred to as Ministering Spirits
    Hebrews 1:14
    The Greek word for "ministering" means "to serve." All angels therefore are *spirit-servants* who come to the aid especially of believers in the out working of God's great purposes on the earth. Praise the Lord!

3. Angels referred to as the Heavenly Host
    II Chronicles 18:18 and I Samuel 17:45; Psalm 89:6, 8
    This seems to be a reference alluding to a rank and order or angels like in a military processional.

4. Angels referred to as God's Holy Ones
    Job 5:1, 15:15; Psalm 89:7; Daniel 4:13, 17, 23; 8:14; Jude 14
    The word holy means 'set apart ones". Yes, God's angels are truly not a part of this worldly system and set apart unto the Lord's work. Acts 7:53, Galatians 3:19, and Hebrews 2:2 all tell us that these "holy ones" brought the Law to God's chosen people. So angels are used to help bring the people of God into a set apart life of holiness unto the Lord! Wow! What a task!

5. Angels referred to as Watchers
    Daniel 4:13; Ezekiel 1:18; Revelation 4:6
    Apparently there are a category of angels who have been sent by God specifically to observe the events taking place on earth. The word "watcher" in Hebrew communicates the idea of being "vigilant, making sleepless watch." Maybe these are God's reconnaissance agents taking pictures and returning with reports to headquarters in heaven. Maybe this is why some angels are referred to being full of eyes!

II. MORE ON THE NATURE OF ANGELS

A. Angels Are Personal Beings
They have mind, will and emotions. Intelligence: II Samuel 14:17 and 20; I Peter 1; 12. Emotions: Hebrews 12:22 – joy; Luke 15:10 – love and rejoice; I Peter 1:12 – desire; Jude 9 and Revelation 12:7 – contend, etc.

B. Angels Are Incorporeal and Invisible
Incorporeal means "lacking material form or substance." It is interesting to note that some Jewish scholars and early Church fathers thought of the angels of having some type of airy or fiery bodies. They do not know what it is like to get old, get ill, and eventually die.

C. Angels Can Appear as Men
According to Matthew 1:20; Luke 1:26; John 20:12, though angels are normally invisible, they can appear as men. Their resemblance can be so realistic that they are at times actually taken to be human beings (Hebrews 13; 2).

D. Angels Have Spatial Limitations
Though they are heavenly spirit beings, they seem to be "localized" and have forms of spatial limitations (but not like ours). They cannot be everywhere at any time. They move from place to place. Daniel 9:21-23 describes Gabriel engaged in "swift flight" to travel from heaven to be by the prophet's side. Awesome!

E. Angels Are Powerful but Not Omnipotent
II Thessalonians 1:7 refers to *"powerful angels"* and Psalm 103:20 call them *"mighty ones who do His bidding."* Matthew 28:2-7 tells about the angels rolling away to giant stone at the sepulcher of Jesus. Some estimate that this wheel of granite could have been 8 feet in diameter and one foot thick making around 8,000 pounds!

Yet, it is clear, though they are great in strength; they are limited and not all powerful as only God Himself is. Angels are no replacement for God! Angels are totally dependent on God and their power is always exercised on behalf of God.

F. Angels Are Obedient
Psalm 103: 20 says the angelic host, *"Praise the Lord, you his angels, you mighty ones who do his bidding, who obey his word."* Angels do not come to do their will – they set an example even for us – they come to do His will on earth as it is done in heaven (see Matt. 6:10).

G. **Angels Are Immortal**

Angels live forever – period. Luke 20:36 clearly states that angels are not subject to death. Once they were created, they have never ceased to exist. Gabriel appeared as mentioned in the Book of Daniel chapter 9. But then this same angel appears 500 years later without having aged as Gabriel to Zechariah, the father of John the Baptist (Luke 1). Over here right now! That's what I say! Over here right now!

III. A LOOK AT CHERUBIM AND SERAPHIM

A. Cherubim

1. Genesis 3:24 – Set to guard the entrance at the Tree of Life.

2. Ark of the Covenant – covering cherubs (Exodus 25:18-22; Hebrews 9:5)

3. II Samuel 22:11a and Psalms 18:4-10 – "And he rode upon a cherub."

4. Thought to have two wings

B. Seraphim

1. Isaiah 6:2, 6 – In the aftermath of the death of good king Uzziah, Isaiah and the entire Jewish nation were feeling insecure, wondering what would happen in the future. The Lord appeared to Isaiah "high and lifted up" and the prophet's spiritual eyes were opened so that the he could see seraphim with six wings. In response to Isaiah's feeling undone a seraphim flew to him with a live coal in his hand from the altar of God in order to purify him.

2. Spoken of as having six wings

3. Cry of the holiness of God is released

IV. OTHER POSSIBILY CATEGORIES OF ANGELS

A. Guardian Angels

Matthew 18:2,10

And He called a child to himself and stood him in their midst ...See that you do not despise one of these little ones, for I say to you, that their angels in heaven continually behold the face of my Father who is in heaven.

B. Four Living Creatures

1. Ezekiel 1:4-28 – Four wings and four faces; notice that they follow the Spirit.

2. Revelation 4:8 – Six wings and four faces are mentioned.

C. Strong Angel

Revelation 5:2 – A strong or mighty angel proclaiming a message from God with a loud voice.

D. Angel with Great Authority

Revelation 18:1 – Perhaps ruling over various territorial spheres with delegated authority.

E. Angel of a Specific Church

1. Revelation 1:20 – the seven stars are the angels of the seven churches.

    Revelation 2 and 3 – Our English word angel comes from the New Testament Greek word, *angelos* meaning messenger or courier.

    There are three different interpretations of what is meant by the term angel in this case.

    a) A literal angel sent from God.
    b) The senior human elder in authority and under God's command.
    c) There are those who believe that it is not an either/or situation but that both realities can be simultaneously true.

V. THE ANGEL OF THE LORD

A. Angel of His Presence

1. Isaiah 63:9 – The angel of his presence saved them out of affliction.

2. Exodus 23:20-23 – The angel of whom God said "for my Name is in him." Supernatural presences were thought to dwell within their name; hence, this angel had God's being dwelling within Him. Perhaps a reference to the pre-existent Son of God before He took human flesh who could then take on the form of an angel.

3. Exodus 33:14-15 – God promised Moses that His presence would go with him and the Israelites to give them rest.

B. Angel of the Lord

1. Theophany – A visible appearance of the Lord Jesus Christ before His incarnation. Before His incarnation as a human being, the Second Person of the Godhead could appear in the form of an angel.

2. Daniel 3 – "The fourth man" who appeared with the three Hebrew worthies in the burning fiery furnace at the time of their great trial to preserve their lives, comforts them, and demonstrates to the prideful pagan King Nebuchadnezzar that God, and not mere man, was in ultimate control of human history.

3. Genesis 18 – Three strangers visited Abram when he was encamped at Mamre. Two of these "men" (verse 22) later went to Sodom and visited Lot to warn him and his family to flee before the impending wrath of God which was to soon be visited upon that unrepentant city. Obviously, angels have the ability to achieve metamorphosis (change shape and form) and materialize or de-materialize at will. They can appear as human beings. Evidently, the Second Person of the Trinity also had this ability before He took on human flesh in the incarnation.

VI. CONCLUSION

The range and extent of the angelic realm is stunning. In spite of our earnest efforts to understand God's Kingdom, we end up with only a partial idea of the infinite variety and unreserved power of these fellow-servants of ours.

Here we have a host of superbly fashioned beings who serve Him (and, by extension, us) with an amazing combination of complete submission to a defined military ranking and complete, joyful liberty. The angels love the way God created them so much that they probably don't evaluate it.–.because their attention is so much on God Himself. They're eager for His next word to them, eager for their next assignment in the service of the Most Holy One.

Father, we call on You to release Your angels right now to places of darkness, where Your fiery ones can shed Your light. May Your kingdom come and Your will be done everywhere on earth as it is in heaven. We see that this world is not a safe place, and we trust that You will send angelic guards to protect us and guide us. May the angels of Your presence be released in our midst. You are the same yesterday, today, and forever. Amen!

Reflection Questions
Lesson Five: The Characteristics of Angels

Answers to these questions can be found in the back of the study guide.

Fill in the Blank

1. The Angel of the Lord was a visible appearance of

   _____ _____.

2. The Ark of the Covenant had covering _____.

3. List five titles given to angels in Scripture:

   a. _____ d. _____

   b. _____ e. _____

   c. _____ g.

Multiple Choice – Choose the best answer from the list below:

A.	Personal	C.	Seraphim
B.	Independent	D.	Cherubim

4. Angels are _____ beings with mind, will, and emotions.

5. In response to Isaiah's feeling undone (Isaiah 6), a _____ flew to him with a live coal in his hand from the altar of God in order to purify him.

True or False

6. Angels do not die, nor do they propagate and give birth to baby angels.

   _____

7. The number of humans on the earth far outweighs the number of angels.

   _____

8. Angels are totally dependent on God and their power is always exercised on behalf of God. _____

Continued on the next page.

Scripture Memorization

9. Write out and memorize Matthew 18:10.

10. Write below two main insights you learned about the characteristics of angels.

Lesson Six:
Angelic Assignments

I. THREE PRIMARY FUNCTIONS OF ANGELS

A. Service to God
Psalms 148:2, 5 – *Praise Him, all His angels: praise Him, all His hosts... Let them praise the name of the Lord: for He commanded, and they were created.*

B. Service to Christians

1. Hebrews 1:7 – *And of the angels he says, "Who makes His angels winds, and his ministers a flame of fire."*

2. Hebrews 1:14 – *Are they not all ministering spirits, sent out to render service for the sake of those who will inherit salvation?*

C. Perform God's Word
The following describes possible ways that angels are released into this dimension of their ministry.

Psalms 103:20, 21 – *Bless the Lord, you His angels, Mighty in strength, who perform His word, obeying the voice of His word! Bless the Lord, all you His hosts, you who serve Him, doing His will.*

1. God's direct command released to the angels giving them a "job to do" or direct assignment.
2. God's command released through His delegate

   a) Through intercession an invitation or request is heard and God then responds to man's cry.
   b) Man hears God's Word in his or her heart and – then gives voice to His Word in a declarative manner. (This could be an example of a rhema word or gift of faith).

II. THE ASSIGNMENTS GIVEN

A. Minister the Presence of God

1. Isaiah 63:9 – *"And the angel of his presence saved them: in His love and in His mercy He redeemed them; and He lifted them and carried them all the days of old."*
2. Revelation 18:1 – Illuminated earth with His glory.

3. Are said to have camped around Charles Finney's meetings.

4. Jim Croft – Pastor in Florida – tells of a counseling session where two angels appeared who released the golden presence of God and those in the room were supernaturally touched by God's presence.

B. Deliver God's Word or Message

1. Matthew 1:20 – Sent to Joseph.

2. Matthew 2:13, 19 – Warnings to take Jesus to Egypt.

3. Luke 1:19, 26 – To Zacharias and then to Mary.

4. Matthew 28:1-7 – Resurrection proclamation.

C. Release Dreams, Revelation and Understanding

1. Daniel 8:15-19 – Understanding of end times imparted.

2. Daniel 9:23 – To gain understanding of the visions granted.

3. Revelation 1:1 – Revelation of Jesus Christ communicated by His angel. This is how the book of Revelation was received by John, the apostle on the Isle of Patmos.

4. A dream given to James Goll pertaining to the ability to interpret dreams and revelation.

D. Guidance and Direction Given

1. Acts 8:26 – Philip and Ethiopian eunuch.

2. Genesis 24:7, 40 – Bride for Isaac.

3. Acts 27:23, 24, 29 – Message to Paul on a ship.

E. Deliverance Brought Forth

1. Isaiah 37:36 – *Then the angel of the Lord went forth, and smote in the camp of the Assyrians a hundred and fourscore and five thousand.*

2. II Kings 19:35 –185,000 of the enemy were struck dead.

3. The British Air Chief Marshall believed that angels drove planes of dead Royal Air Force pilots during the Battle of Britain during World War II and thus helped protect Britain from Nazi invasion.

F. Protection Granted

1. Matthew 18:10 – Guardians over children.

2. Psalms 91:11, 12 – In charge over believers, bearing us up from danger.

3. Psalms 34:7 – Encamps *"round about"* surrounding and delivering those who fear God.

G. Death of the Saints

1. Psalms 116:15 – Precious is the death of His godly ones.

2. Psalms 23:4 – In *"the valley of the shadow of death, Thou art with me."*

3. Luke 16:22 – Lazarus carried away by the angels

4. Jude 9 – Dispute over Moses' body was made between the God's and the powers of darkness.

H. Impart Strength

1. Matthew 4:11 – After a 40 day fast, they imparted strength to Jesus.

2. Luke 22:43 – Jesus in Gethsemane was once again strengthened supernaturally.

3. Daniel 10:16-18 – During a time of distress angels were used to impart God's strength.

I. Releasing Healing

1. John. 5:4 – *At the pool of Bethesda, an angel would stir the waters and healing would occur.*

2. William Branham's testimony – May 7, 1946 – An angel appeared to him imparting gifts of healing and the gift of the word of knowledge.[14]

The angel said to Branham, "Fear not. I am sent from the Presence of Almighty God to tell you that your peculiar life and your misunderstood ways have been to indicate that God has sent you to take a gift of divine healing to the peoples of the world. If you will be sincere and get the people to believe you, nothing shall stand before your prayer...not even cancer!"

The angel went on to tell William Branham that he would take the ministry of healing around the world and eventually pray for kings, princes and monarchs. Brother Branham responded by saying, "how can this be since I am a poor man and I live among poor people and I have no education." The angel then continued the commission saying, "as the prophet Moses was given two signs to prove that he was sent from God, so will you be given two signs."

For approximately 30 minutes the angel stood before Bro. Branham explaining the commission and the way the ministry would operate in the supernatural arena. [15]

III. DO IT AGAIN!

What God did before, He will do again. So we welcome the angels of the Lord to release His manifested presence, to deliver God's Word, release dreams, visions and interpret revelation.

We want to be Wind Blown Believers as stated in John 3 who know the sound of the wind and catch it. Release your winds – your angels – to help grant us guidance and direction. Protect and guard us, watch over us in all our ways. Walk with us through the hard times and the good. Come near us and our loved ones as we cross the threshold from the temporal into the eternal.

Impart supernatural strength and might to us to do the task well. Energize us for Jesus Christ sake. May the pools of Bethesda be stirred up in our lives to bring healing to others. Release angels to come and change the culture of our sphere of influence. We welcome heavens army into the earth realm. Amen!

Reflection Questions
Lesson Six: Angelic Assignments

Answers to these questions can be found in the back of the study guide.

Fill in the Blank

1. What are three primary functions of angels?

    a. _____

    b. _____

    c. _____

2. _____ fought and prevailed against the fallen angelic principality over Persia in response to Daniel's _____.

Multiple Choice – Choose the best answer from the list below:

A.	Harvest	C.	Messages
B.	Strength	D.	Creation

3. Angels deliver God's _____ on the earth.

4. Angels can impart supernatural _____.

True or False

5. Angels can release dreams, revelation, and understanding. _____

6. Angels have the power to kill humans. _____

Continued on the next page.

Scripture Memorization

7. Write out and memorize Isaiah 63:9.

Reflection and Journaling

8. Review the 19 assignments given to angels from Section II. Pray through each one asking the Lord to assign His angels to advance His Kingdom in these specific ways. Write down what the Holy Spirit speaks to you below and on the next page.

Lesson Seven:
Jesus and the Ministering Angels

I.   I LOVE TO TELL THE STORY

A.   Thoughts from Colossians 1:16

Paul, the beloved apostle, gave us great insight in Colossians 1:16, *"For by Him all things were created, both in the heavens and on earth, visible and invisible, whether thrones or dominions or rulers or authorities – all things have been created through Him and for Him."*

Jesus created all things, all spheres, and all powers. All things created both in heaven and in earth have the same ultimate purpose: to serve God's purposes and to give Him glory!

B.   I Timothy 3:14-16

Paul gave us the following short but unique rendition of the
Gospel message.

I am writing these things to you, hoping to come to you before long; but in case I am delayed, I write so that you will know how one ought to conduct himself in the household of God, which is the church of the living God, the pillar and support of the truth. By common confession, great is the mystery of godliness:

> *He who was revealed in the flesh,*
> *Was vindicated in the Spirit,*
> *Seen by angels,*
> *Proclaimed among the nations,*
> *Believed on in the world,*
> *Taken up in glory.*

II.   WORSHIPPING THE PREINCARNATE CHRIST

Isaiah 6:1-5

Some 700 years before the birth of Jesus at Bethlehem, in approximately 740 B.C., we find the prophet Isaiah in worship in the Temple. He was possibly mourning the death of King Uzziah. While there, Isaiah received angelic encounters, but ultimately his total attention was given to the one who was "high and lifted up" and whose glory filled the house.

As the veil between the temporal and eternal was parted, Isaiah was shown the worship of heaven including the burning seraphs who cried, *"Holy, holy, holy is the Lord Almighty."* These angels covered their faces with their wings as an act of humility and worship. But perhaps there is more here. The New Testament tells us (I Timothy 6:16) that God dwells in "unapproachable light". Despite the incredible brightness that emanated from these angels themselves, they had to hide themselves in part from the radiant piercing presence of light of God who is altogether holy!

This is but one of many pictures given to us of the angels in heaven worshipping the preincarnate Christ. Indeed, it is awesome!

III. PROCLAMING THE BIRTH OF CHRIST

A. Declaring the Birth to Mary – Luke 1: 26-38
Gabriel makes a pronouncement to Mary that she has found favor with God, she will be with child, and that His Name would be called Jesus – meaning "the Lord saves" or "the Lord is our salvation."

Mary then responds by asking how this will be since I am a virgin (verse 34). Then verses 35 through 37 then records the most amazing conversation between this messenger angel and Mary, the one chosen. Mary believes and cries out, *"Be it unto me according to your word"* (Luke 1:38).

B. Announcing the Birth to Joseph – Matthew 1:19-21, 24-25 (NIV)
Because Joseph her husband was a righteous man and did not want to expose her to public disgrace, he had in mind to divorce her quietly. But after he had considered this, an angel of the Lord appeared to him in a dream and said, "Joseph son of David, do not be afraid to take Mary home as your wife, because what is conceived in her is from the Holy Spirit. She will give birth to a son, and you are to give him the name Jesus, because he will save his people from their sins."

...When Joseph woke up, he did what the angel of the Lord had commanded him and took Mary home as his wife. But he had no union with her until she gave birth to a son. And he gave him the name Jesus.

C. Addressing the Arrival to the Shepherds – Luke 2:8-14 (KJV)
And there were in the same country shepherds abiding in the field, keeping watch over their flock by night. And, lo, the angel of the Lord came upon them, and the glory of the Lord shone round about them: and they were sore afraid. And the angel said unto them, Fear not: for, behold, I bring you good tidings of great joy, which shall be to all people. For unto you is born this day in the city of David a Saviour,

which is Christ the Lord. And this shall be a sign unto you; Ye shall find the babe wrapped in swaddling clothes, lying in a manger. And suddenly there was with the angel a multitude of the heavenly host praising God, and saying, Glory to God in the highest, and on earth peace, good will toward men.

IV. MINISTERING TO JESUS WHILE ON EARTH

A. His Early Infancy of Christ – Matthew 2:13-20

B. His Wilderness Experience – Matthew 4:11
Then the devil left Him; and behold, angels came and began to minister to Him

C. His Gethsemane Experience – Luke 22:43 (Amplified)
There appeared to Him an angel from heaven, strengthening Him in spirit.

D. His Crucifixion Experience – Matthew 26:52-54
Then Jesus said to him, "Put your sword back into its place, for all who draw the sword will die by the sword. Do you suppose that I cannot appeal to My Father, and He will immediately provide Me with more than twelve legions [more than 80,000] of angels? But how then would the Scriptures be fulfilled, that it must come about this way?"

V. SERVING AT THE RESSURECTION AND ASCENSION OF JESUS

A. Serving at His Resurrection – Matthew 28:1-9 (Amplified)
Now after the Sabbath, near dawn of the first day of the week, Mary of Magdala and the other Mary went to take a look at the tomb. And behold, there was a great earthquake, for an angel of the Lord descended from heaven and came and rolled the boulder back and sat upon it. His appearance was like lightning, and his garments as white as snow. And those keeping guard were so frightened at the sight of him that they were agitated and they trembled and became like dead men. But the angel said to the women, "Do not be alarmed and frightened, for I know that you are looking for Jesus, Who was crucified. He is not here; He has risen, as He said [He would do]. Come; see the place where He lay. Then go quickly and tell His disciples, He has risen from the dead, and behold, He is going before you to Galilee; there you will see Him. Behold, I have told you".

So they left the tomb hastily with fear and great joy and ran to tell the disciples. And as they went, behold, Jesus met them and said, Hail (greetings)! And they went up to Him and clasped His feet and worshiped Him.

B. Serving at His Ascension – Acts 1:8-11

"But you will receive power when the Holy Spirit has come upon you; and you shall be My witnesses both in Jerusalem, and in all Judea and Samaria, and even to the remotest part of the earth."

And after He had said these things, He was lifted up while they were looking on, and a cloud received Him out of their sight. And as they were gazing intently into the sky while He was going, behold, two men in white clothing stood beside them. They also said, "Men of Galilee, why do you stand looking into the sky? This Jesus, who has been taken up from you into heaven, will come in just the same way as you have watched Him go into heaven."

VI. DESCENDING AT THE SECOND COMING

The scriptures declare that when the Lord Jesus Christ returns to earth visibly and physically He will be accompanied by a host of angels. Consider:

A. Matthew 16:27

"For the Son of Man is going to come in the glory of His Father with His angels...."

B. Matthew 25:31

"But when the Son of Man comes in His glory, and all the angels with Him, then He will sit on His glorious throne."

C. II Thessalonians 1:6-8

For after all it is only just for God to repay with affliction those who afflict you, and to give relief to you who are afflicted and to us as well when the Lord Jesus will be revealed from heaven with His mighty angels in flaming fire, dealing out retribution to those who do not know God and to those who do not obey the gospel of our Lord Jesus.

VII. EXALTING CHRIST FOREVER

One of the greatest ministries of angels is that of worship. They begin there, they do throughout the ages, and they end up doing this one magnificent thing throughout all eternity. They worship God! Angels exalt the Lamb.

Revelation 5:11-6:1

Then I looked, and I heard the voice of many angels around the throne and the living creatures and the elders; and the number of them was myriads of myriads, and thousands of thousands, saying with a loud voice, "Worthy is the Lamb that was slain to receive power and riches and wisdom and might and honor and glory and blessing." And every created thing which is in heaven and on the earth and under the earth and on the sea, and all things in them, I heard saying, "To Him who sits on the throne, and to the Lamb, be blessing and honor and glory and dominion forever and ever." And the four living creatures kept saying, "Amen." And the elders fell down and worshipped.

Let us call out to God – that He would open our eyes to gaze upon what the angels see and worship the Lamb who is most worthy!

Reflection Questions
Lesson Seven: Jesus and the Ministering Angels

Answers to these questions can be found in the back of the study guide.

Fill in the Blank

1. Angels worshipped the _____ Christ.

2. List four occasions that angels ministered to Jesus while He was on earth.

    a. _____

    b. _____

    c. _____

    d. _____

Multiple Choice – Choose the best answer from the list below:

A.	Worship	C.	Power
B.	Warfare	D.	Angels

3. One of the greatest ministries of angels is that of _____.

4. Jesus Christ is going to come in the glory of His Father with His _____.

True or False

5. When the Lord Jesus Christ returns to earth visibly and physically, He will be accompanied by a host of angels. _____

6. God dwells in "unapproachable light" so that even brilliant angels have to hide themselves in part from the radiant, piercing presence of God. _____

Continued on the next page.

Scripture Memorization

7. Write out and memorize Colossians 1:16.

Reflection and Prayer

8. Read and reflect upon Revelation 5:11-6:1. Then take time to pray passionately through these verses, specifically joining with the declaration of the angels around the throne.

Lesson Eight:
Modern-Day Reports of Angelic Encounters
(Michal Ann Goll)

I. INTRODUCTION

"Can you imagine a being, white and dazzling as lighting? General William Booth, founder of the Salvation Army, described a vision of angelic beings, stating that every angel was surrounded with an aura of rainbow light so brilliant that were it not withheld, no human being could stand the sight of it."[16]

II. "ENTRANCE TO RAVENSBRUCK" – CORRIE TEN BOOM

Corrie ten Boom was a Dutch woman who was arrested by the Nazis during World War II for hiding Jews and who became famous later in her life because of her book and a film, both called *The Hiding Place.* Corrie and her sister Betsie were transferred from a concentration camp in the Netherlands to the infamous Ravensbrück camp in Germany. After they had been unloaded from the train that had brought them to Germany, they were being processed, herded like cattle, along with a crowd of women prisoners. Corrie tells what happened:

"Together we entered the terrifying building. At a table were women who took away all our possessions. Everyone had to undress completely and then go to a room where her hair was checked.

"I asked a woman who was busy checking the possessions of the new arrivals if I might use the toilet. She pointed to a door, and I discovered that the convenience was nothing more than a hole in the shower room floor. Betsie stayed close beside me all the time. Suddenly I had an inspiration, "Quick, take off your woolen underwear," I whispered to her. I rolled it up with mine and laid the bundle in a corner with my little Bible. The spot was alive with cockroaches, but I didn't worry about that. I felt wonderfully relieved and happy....

"We hurried back to the row of women waiting to be undressed. A little later, after we had had our showers and put on our shirts and shabby dresses, I hid the roll of underwear and my Bible under my dress. It did bulge out obviously through my dress; but I prayed, "Lord, cause now Thine angels to surround me; and let them not be transparent today, for the guards must not see me." I felt perfectly at ease. Calmly I passed the guards. Everyone was checked, from the front, the sides, and the back. Not a bulge escaped the eyes of the guard. The woman just in front of me had hidden a woolen vest under her dress; it was taken from her. They let me pass, for they did not see me. Betsie, right behind me, was searched."

But outside awaited another danger. On each side of the door were women who looked everyone over for a second time. They felt over the body of each one who passed. I knew they would not see me, for the angels were still surrounding me. I was not even surprised when they passed me by; but within me rose the jubilant cry, "O Lord, if Thou dost so answer prayer, I can face even Ravensbrück unafraid."[17]

III. "AN EXTRA MEASURE" – LEON HOOVER

Leon and Paula Hoover have been partnering with our ministry for a few years, but before they came to Tennessee, they served as missionaries in West Africa. While they were there, they experienced a time of great trials. Leon and his daughter Natalie had fallen very sick, and yet he and Paula tried to keep up with their duties. They also had a young son named Luke. Because of the sickness, the family was having difficulty sleeping through the night, all in one room of their little house. In Leon's words:

"We had learned early on in our stay that visiting the sick is an important part of life in West Africa. Our house had been crowded with people wanting to simply *be* with me during my sickness.

"After the evening chores, most of which were done by Paula, we again quickly made our rounds among the huts to excuse ourselves for not sitting around their fire and sharing their food. They were always so gracious, but we could tell they felt badly for us.

"That night, we did sleep. I awoke very peacefully around 4:00 A.M. Realizing we had all been asleep since well before midnight, I began thanking Jesus for His faithfulness and for this precious gift of peaceful rest. I was so grateful. As I prayed, I drifted off into a deep sleep again. So it was that I didn't really see or hear him come in....

"Groggy from my first peaceful night's rest, I couldn't quite understand what was going on. *Who was this, and what did he want that couldn't wait until the sun was up?*

"The inside of our mud brick home was as dark as a cave during the night. With the window and door shut to keep out the bats, I could hardly see my hand in front of my face. But behind him, the tin door to the exterior hung ajar on its hinges, so that the moonlight drifted inside to outline his silhouette. Sitting there on his heels, he filled the width and a good portion of the five-foot-high doorway into our sleeping chamber. Otherwise, I might not have seen him at all.

"He was big, bigger than the men I had seen at Yenderé. Yet he was dressed much like them, wearing a tattered sleeveless shirt and pants, much like the ones used when working in the fields. He was squatting quietly on his heels at the foot of our cots. Breathing rapidly like an athlete after a track event, he seemed winded, though not tired. I was not surprised by that; all the men around there were in excellent physical condition.... It seemed he had traveled a great distance or had hurried to get here. *But, why?*

'It's good you're sleeping well,' he said. 'Yes, I'm very grateful,' I replied.

"In his big brown hands, he held a large gourd bowl. I had seen it when I realized he was in the hut. In the back of my mind, I hoped it wasn't full of that corn flour drink. But I figured if he had bothered to come at this hour of the morning, I ought to be polite enough to accept whatever he offered.

"He produced a large metal spoon. I couldn't really see from where; perhaps it had been inside his open shirt. As he slowly stirred the contents of the bowl, I began to wake up enough to wonder just what was going on. *Who was this guy?* He was huge, and I didn't recognize him as being part of the village. My eyes had adjusted enough to discern the definition of his muscles. His breathing rate had already slowed. It was nearly back to normal and he seemed so pleased... *Why was that?* But he was saying something else. *What was it?*

'We were on our way from the beginning, but there was some trouble. It was...'
'You mean there was a fight?' I interrupted. 'A fight? Then you must...'
'Merely a delay,' he continued. 'There was some opposition to our coming, but that's settled. We're here now and that's why you sleep well.'

"When I first saw him, I had wondered why his presence had not startled me. Now, however, it was apparent whose messenger he was. I knew that whatever he had in that bowl for me, I should accept. No more words were needed. He dipped the spoon into the bowl and held it to my mouth. I swallowed it all. Though it seemed a familiar substance, it was rather like nothing at all going down. There wasn't much taste and not much to say about its consistency either. I couldn't place it. I was relieved, though, and glad to have taken my spoonful.

"I awoke Paula, Luke, and Natalie, telling them they needed to take a spoonful of this. We were all sitting cross-legged on our cots in a semicircle around the visitor squatting in the doorway. I was concerned that Luke and Natalie might not take the drink. "Each of you need to take this," I said. He gave each of them a spoonful, dipping into the gourd and putting the spoon to their lips just as he had for me. I watched them lie down again and when I turned toward the door, he was gone. He had gone out as quietly and peacefully as he had come in.

"It was around 5:30 before I awoke again. As the morning light slipped under the edges of the straw roof, I could hear the village coming to life. I lay there pondering the experience. I had never been visited by an angel, much less talked with one. *Had it been more than a dream? Had I been awake? And that bowl, what exactly had he given us?*

"Luke, Natalie, and Paula awoke soon. As they were getting dressed, I sat on my cot and recounted to Luke the angel's coming, as Natalie and Paula listened closely. It was during the retelling of it that I realized what he had given us."

Leon goes on to recount how his condition and Natalie's grew worse as the day went on. Thanks to the loan of a moped, all four of them were able to reach a medical clinic in a bigger town, and, through a series of God-ordained "coincidences," eventually to a mission hospital in the neighboring country of Cote d'Ivoire. Leon and Natalie seemed to be suffering from malaria.

Even with medical treatment, Leon's condition grew so serious that "death did not seem a remote possibility." So early one morning in the hospital, he set his spiritual house in order, writing individual letters to his wife and the two children, adding one for the unborn child that he and Paula suspected she was carrying. He tucked the letters into his Bible.

Within a week, however, he was well enough to return to them, although he was weak and he had lost more than 25 pounds. So Leon and Paula kept taking care of their family and working. (They were in training as missionaries.) Over time, Leon suffered several relapses. Finally, medical personnel decided that he must be fighting more than malaria, and tests in another hospital in Lomé revealed hepatitis B as well as typhoid fever and a severe infestation of giardia. He had to stay in Lomé for nearly three months, with most of it on complete bed rest. This was very difficult indeed on the whole family.

On top of everything else, Paula did turn out to be pregnant, but she lost the baby, most likely because of the anti-malaria drugs she had been taking. They clung to their faith in God and He kept them from sinking into complete discouragement.

What had been in the bowl? What had the angel given them to drink? Leon writes,

The bowl the angel had brought us was full of *faith,* "the substance of things hoped for, the evidence of things not seen" [Heb. 11:1, KJV]. The angel had been sent to give us each an extra measure of faith....

We surely needed that extra measure of faith, because ours was running low. The light within us had grown dim; the beast of impossibility was ready to take us. Somehow though, with God's grace, we managed to [put] that behind us.

God's grace. The fear of the Lord. Those were household expressions for us back in Georgia [in the States, before they came to Africa]. Now we tremble with respect, adoration, and love at the thought of the awesome and holy God we serve.

The angel provided *faith,* which was exactly what the Hoovers needed. Once he had delivered that, they used their extra measure of faith to get through that difficult season and, even as they do now, to continue to step over impossibilities.

IV. "I SMELL CHOCOLATE!" – BILL YOUNT

Hershey, Pennsylvania, as most people know, is famous because of the Hershey Chocolate Company, and is named after candy-maker and philanthropist Milton Hershey (1857-1945). Milton Hershey's wife Catherine couldn't have children, and she suffered from a deteriorating muscular disease. Her situation motivated her husband to establish a school for financially needy children, the Milton Hershey School, and to become involved in medical research. Through the Milton Hershey School Trust, a medical research hospital and medical school, now part of the University of Pennsylvania, were established. All the Hershey endeavors are flourishing to this day.

Bill Yount was in prayer about Hershey, Pennsylvania, and he overheard the messages of some angels—both fallen and unfallen ones:

"I saw one of the greatest outpourings of healing being erected as a healing zone, invading and surrounding the community of Hershey, Pennsylvania. I heard a strong angel decreeing: "And there shall be 'drive thru' healings taking place in this city and surrounding its borders.""

"Then I heard the enemy complaining and regretting the days that the womb of Milton Hershey's wife could not conceive. "Now we have a 'womb of healing' opening up in this place, where multitudes will conceive their healing for the nations." I heard the stronghold spirit over Hershey crying out to hell, "It's Hershey; we've got a problem!""

"I saw the angels of orphans and underprivileged children standing before the face of the Father, bringing their cries of "Abba, Father," and their tears for Daddy to come home to Hershey to be with them. And I heard the Father dispatching something like a news alert back to these orphans and children, "I'll be there with bells on! I am coming to bless the day Milton Hershey blessed my orphaned, fatherless children. I am coming to bless the whole town, city, and beyond its borders! ... I am turning the hearts of the children to their fathers and the hearts of the fathers to their children.""

"I saw angels dropping cures for diseases into the Hershey Medical Center. Unknown sicknesses and diseases were being given names, and angels were dropping these names down, and cures were following behind them to be released to the world.

"Then I heard the enemy proclaiming throughout all of hell: "We have been working overtime to stop those praying Christians and to bring division to those churches and families, but we have overlooked the power of the cries of the fatherless! Those cries were coming from outside of the church and ascending straight to the throne of their real Father. And He's coming to Hershey with full force.""

"As a sweet-smelling aroma ascended from Hershey, Pennsylvania to the throne, I heard trembling words come screaming from hell, *"I smell chocolate. I smell milk. I smell honey. It smells like the Promised Land!"* [18]

V. SIX MONTH'S NOTICE – ROLAND BUCK FROM *ANGELS ON ASSIGNMENT* [19]

While Roland was in heaven, God allowed him to see what was going to happen six months before a couple with serious marital problems entered his office. Below is a summary of Roland's account:

"While I was in heaven, I saw them coming into my office and noticed the date on the paper on which day this was to occur. When this date arrived, these particular people didn't show up and I wondered what happened. So I decided to stay a little while longer at my office. A short time after my normal closing hour the telephone rang and a person who didn't identify himself asked, "Pastor Buck, will you be in your office for a little while?" I said, "Yes." He didn't tell me who he was.

"When they came to the door, I greeted them by name. This really shook them up. Then I asked, "What brought you here?" They said that they had been having terrible marital problems and decided they had to go somewhere to clear the air. They didn't know why, but they had decided to come to Boise, Idaho. "We drove up here, rented a hotel room, and when we got inside the room we noticed the telephone book was lying open to the spot where you have your ad, which reads, 'Counseling by appointment.'"

"Instantly I knew that one of those angels had been there ahead of time and had opened the directory to the right place and had also arranged at the front desk for them to get the right room. As we conversed the lady said, "We have had a good time driving up here together. Things are all straightened out and everything is going to be all right. So we don't want to waste your time. We'll be leaving now."

"I said, "No, you had better stay here because that isn't the way it is." I told them that God had let me see this event months before. I said to the wife, "You have a gun in your purse and you are planning to shoot your husband as soon as you get back to your motel." He was really alarmed and exclaimed, "You'd better not shoot me!" She was shaking all over. Then I said, "Open your purse and give me that gun." She opened her purse and gave me the gun, just as I had seen it before.

"Then her very soul cried out to God. She knew there was no way I could have known anything about the gun unless God had told me. And He had let me know about it almost six months before it happened.

"Immediately both of them fell down on their faces before God. He washed their sins away and instantly put their marriage back together. I have had one beautiful letter from them since then. They are going to a good church in California, happy in the Lord and serving God."

Reflection Questions
Lesson Eight: Modern-Day Reports of Angelic Encounters

Answers to these questions can be found in the back of the study guide.

Reflection and Journaling

1. Reflect on each of the four stories you read. For each story, journal your response to the following:

   • How did an angel uniquely serve this person?

   • Draw specific comparisons between this story and what you've learned about angels in Lessons 4-7.

   "Entrance to Ravensbruck" – Corrie ten Boom

   "An Extra Measure" – Leon and Paula Hoover

Continued on the next page.

<u>"I Smell Chocolate!" – Bill Yount</u>

<u>"Six Months' Notice" – Roland Buck</u>

2. What is the main insight you received from these stories?

Lesson Nine:
Discerning the Angelic Presence

I. THE GIFT OF DISCERNING OF SPIRITS

A. The Gift of the Holy Spirit – I Corinthians 12:4-11

*Now there are varieties of gifts, but the same Spirit. And there are varieties of ministries, and the same Lord. There are varieties of effects, but the same God who works all things in all persons. But to each one is given the manifestation of the Spirit for the common good. For to one is given the word of wisdom through the Spirit, and to another the word of knowledge according to the same Spirit; to another faith by the same Spirit, and to another gifts of healing by the one Spirit, and to another the effecting of miracles, and to another prophecy, and to another the **distinguishing of spirits**, to another various kinds of tongues, and to another the interpretation of tongues. But one and the same Spirit works all these things, distributing to each one individually just as He wills* (emphasis added).

The word "discern" means to perceive, distinguish or differentiate. A gift of the Holy Spirit enables one to know what the true source is of the spiritual operation behind an activity. This gift will peer into the various classifications of "spirits" whether they are angelic, demonic, of the human spirit, or of the Holy Spirit.

B. Discerning of Angels – Quoted from *The Seer*

Discerning of spirits also involves discerning of angels, because they are spiritual beings. Jesus saw an angel while He was praying in the Garden of Gethsemane: He knelt down and began to pray, saying, *"Father, if You are willing, remove this cup from Me; yet not My will, but Yours be done." Now an angel from heaven appeared to Him, strengthening Him* (Luke 22:41-43).

The text does not say how Jesus saw the angel, whether in the spiritual realm alone or in full bodily appearance, but He was strengthened by the angel's presence. No one can see angels unless God enables it through the seer dimension of the gift of discernment. He releases things for a purpose. If God enables us to see – whether angels or anything else – it is for a reason, and we need to search out that reason.

On the day of Jesus' resurrection, Mary Magdalene saw two angels when she visited the empty tomb: "But Mary was standing outside the tomb weeping; and so, as she wept, she stooped and looked into the tomb; and she saw two angels in white sitting, one at the head and one at the feet, where the body of Jesus had been lying. And they said to her, "Woman, why are you weeping?"... (John 20:11-13a)

Did Mary see these angels with her natural eye or in the realm of the spirit? How did she know they were angels? The text does not say. Let it suffice that Mary had a spiritual experience in which she discerned the presence of angels.

These angels came to point Mary in a new direction. She came looking for Jesus' body. They came to prepare her to meet her risen Lord, which she did immediately after this encounter. *Seeing Jesus in the garden, Mary thought at first that He was the gardener. Upon recognizing Him at last, she fell at His feet in worship. Later, she went to the disciples and proclaimed, "I have seen the Lord"* (John 20:18).

God sent angels to direct Mary to see Jesus as He really was rather than as she thought He was. Sometimes, if needed, He will do the same for us to correct our vision so that we can get rid of false impressions and see our Lord as He really is.

Paul also saw an angel. In the middle of a great storm at sea, an angelic envoy delivered a message of hope and encouragement for the apostle and all who were on the ship with him. The next day, Paul shared his vision with the others: *"Yet now I urge you to keep up your courage, for there will be no loss of life among you, but only of the ship. For this very night an angel of the God to whom I belong and whom I serve stood before me, saying, 'Do not be afraid, Paul; you must stand before Caesar; and behold, God has granted you all those who are sailing with you"* (Acts 27:22-24).

Was Paul dreaming, or did he have an open vision? No one really knows. The important thing is the message the angel brought that was fulfilled just as promised. In the end, the ship ran aground and was beaten apart by the waves, but everyone aboard made it safely to land.

II. THREE SCRIPTURAL WARNINGS

Among the 300 scriptures on angels we find three main warnings concerning angelic beings. Let's look at them:

A. Do Not Worship
Colossians 2:18, 19 – *Let no man beguile you of your reward in a voluntary humility and worshipping of angels, intruding into those things which he hath no seen, vainly puffed up by his fleshly mind.*

B. Do Not Revile

1. Jude 8 – *Likewise also these filthy dreamers defile the flesh, despise dominion, and speak evil of dignities.*

2. II Pet. 2:10, 11 – *But chiefly them that walk after the flesh in the lust of uncleanness, and despise government. Presumptuous are they, self-willed, they are not afraid to speak evil of dignities. Whereas angels, which are greater in power and might, bring not railing accusation against them before the Lord.*

C. Judge Message
Galatians 1:8 – *But though we, or an angel from heaven, preach any other gospel unto you than that, which we have preached unto you, let him be accursed.*

III. TRYING THE SPIRITS

A. Testing the Spirits
We must learn to try or test the spirits. Discernment is desperately needed in the Body of Christ today! We need a clear release of revelatory activity in our day. John, the beloved apostle of Jesus warns believers of every age: *Beloved, do not believe every spirit, but test the spirits to see whether they are from God; because many false prophets have gone out into the world. By this you know the Spirit of God: every spirit that confesses that Jesus Christ has come in the flesh is from God; and every spirit that does not confess Jesus is not from God; and this is the spirit of the antichrist, of which you have heard that it is coming, and now it is already in the world* (I John 4:1-3).

B. The Necessity of Testing the Spirits

We have to test the spirits because the scripture admonishes us to do so. That is good enough reason – period. But there is also a great increase of the realms of the occult, familiar spirits, witchcraft and other seducing and deceiving spirits as the true and authentic is genuinely on the rise.

God's Word tells us that we must, *"prove all things and hold fast to that which is good"* (I Thessalonians 5:21). The fact that revelation is open for judgment in this age proves its present and imperfect state. But remember the imperfect state of revelation is directly linked to the imperfect state of the people who deliver it – not to an imperfect God! After all, all the gifts of the Holy Spirit are delivered through imperfect people.

Evil and deceived false prophets are not the major source of erroneous accounts to God's people today. Though this is on the rise, the vast majority of "diluted stuff" comes from people who to tend of add their own insights to what started out as authentic, God-birthed encounter. Let's not cheapen the authentic by promoting something as if it is a higher level than it really is.

C. Be Aware of Seducing and Familiar Spirits

1. I Timothy 4:1
    "But the Spirit explicitly says that in later times some will fall away from the faith, paying attention to deceitful spirits and doctrines of demons...."

    A seducing or deceiving demonic spirit is an evil emissary sent from the dark side to perform a certain mission. That is mission is to entice, lure, attract, arouse, fascinate etc. a certain person and bring them from a place of stability into a place of captivity. This spirit then often turns that person over to other demonic spirits to continue their dark work. Thus, a seducing spirit is often a demonic forerunner paving the way for a host of other demonic gangs to come into play. Ultimately, these seducing spirits sear the conscience "as with a hot iron."

2. Deuteronomy 18:9-12

When thou art come into the land which the LORD thy God giveth thee, thou shalt not learn to do after the abominations of those nations. There shall not be found among you any one that maketh his son or his daughter to pass through the fire, or that useth divination, or an observer of times, or an enchanter, or a witch, or a charmer, or a consulter with familiar spirits, or a wizard, or a necromancer. For all that do these things are an abomination unto the LORD: and because of these abominations the LORD thy God doth drive them out from before thee. KJV

The term "familiar" is used here and in I Samuel 28: 3, 7, 8 and in Leviticus 19:27, 31 to describe a particular demonic spirit that takes on the form of a physical body often that of a relative or someone known to the individual. It pertains to the "family" or "familiar" meaning "well known". These false apparitions also may attempt to appear as a "messenger of God" bringing a word of the Lord.

3. Adaptive Deception

Just be on the alert that shift shaping demonic spirits or fallen angels might attempt to impersonate a deceased loved one, even a biblical figure or attempt to appear as a true angelic messenger. These entities may appear in one generation in one form and then adaptive in any other generation in another form but still with the same ultimate purpose: to deceive and capture.

D.   Nine Scriptural Tests

The following is a list of nine scriptural tests we can apply to all spiritual activity that we receive for accuracy, authority, and validity. The following truths are for all of us – whether you are a seasoned prophetic voice or everyday believer in the Lord Jesus Christ.

1. Does the revelation edify, exhort, or console? *But one who prophesies speaks to men for edification and exhortation and consolation* (I Corinthians 14:3, emphasis added). The end result of all true encounters is to build up, to admonish, and to encourage the people of God. Anything that is not directed to this end is not authentic of the Holy Spirit. Jeremiah the prophet had to fulfill a negative commission, but even his difficult message contained a powerful and positive promise of God for those who were obedient (Jeremiah 1:5, 10). I Corinthians 14:26c sums it up best: *Let all things be done unto edification.*

2. Is it in agreement with God's Word? *All scripture is given by inspiration of God* (II Tim. 3:16a, KJV). Authentic God encounters agree with the intent and the spirit of Scripture (II Corinthians 1:17-20). Where the Holy Spirit says "Yes and amen" in Scripture, He also says "Yes and amen" in revelation. He never contradicts Himself.

3. Does it exalt Jesus Christ? *He shall glorify Me; for He shall take of Mine, and shall disclose it to you* (John 16:14). All true spiritual experience ultimately centers on Jesus Christ, and exalts and glorifies Him (Revelation 19:10).

4. Does it have good fruit? *Beware of false prophets, who come to you in sheep's clothing, but inwardly are ravenous wolves. You will know them by their fruits* (Matthew 7:15-16). True spiritual activity produces fruit in character and conduct that agrees with the fruit of the Holy Spirit (Ephesians 5:9; Galatians 5:22-23). Some of the aspects of character that clearly are not the fruit of the Holy Spirit include pride, arrogance, boastfulness, exaggeration, dishonesty, covetousness, financial irresponsibility, licentiousness, immorality, addictive appetites, broken marriage vows, and broken homes. Normally, any revelation or encounter that is responsible for these kinds of results is from a source other than the Holy Spirit.

5. If it predicts a future event, does it come to pass? (Deuteronomy 18:20-22) Any experience that gives a prediction concerning the future should come to pass. If it does not, then, with a few exceptions, the revelation is a mixture or is not from God. Exceptions may include the following issues:

    a. Will of person involved.
    b. National repentance—Ninevah repented, so the word did not occur.
    c. Messianic predictions. (They took hundreds of years to fulfill).
    d. There is a different standard for New Testament prophets than for Old Testament prophets whose predictions played into God's Messianic plan of deliverance.

6. Does the prophetic prediction turn people toward God or away from Him? (Deuteronomy 13:1-5) The fact that a being releases a prediction concerning the future that is fulfilled does not necessarily mean that messenger is sent from God though. If the

eventual outcome is that the experience is used to turn others away from obedience to God, then that experience is false—even if correct predictions concerning the future are included.

7. Does it produce liberty or bondage? "For you have not received a spirit of slavery leading to fear again, but you have received a spirit of adoption as sons by which we cry out, 'Abba! Father!'" (Romans 8:15) True revelation given by the Holy Spirit produces liberty, not bondage (I Corinthians 14:33; II Timothy 1:7). The Holy Spirit never makes believers act like slaves, nor does He ever manipulate us by fear or legalistic compulsion.

8. Does it produce life or death? *Who also made us adequate as servants of a new covenant, not of the letter, but of the Spirit; for the letter kills, but the Spirit gives life* (II Corinthians 3:6). True God encounters from produce life, not death.

9. Does the Holy Spirit bear witness that it is true? *And as for you, the anointing which you received from Him abides in you, and you have no need for anyone to teach you; but as His anointing teaches you about all things and is true and is not a lie, and just as it has taught you, you abide in Him* (I John 2:27). The Holy Spirit within the believer always bears witness or confirms when it is true visitation or spiritual experience. After all, the Holy Spirit is "the Spirit of Truth" (John 16:13). He bears witness to that which is true and He rejects that which is false. This last test is the most subjective of all them all. For that reason, this test must be used along with other previous eight more objective guidelines.

IV. BIBLICAL AND EXPERIENTIAL WAYS

A. According to Scripture

1. I Heard...
    Daniel 8:15-17 – *And it came about when I, Daniel, had seen the vision, that I sought to understand it; and behold, standing before me was one who looked like a man. And I heard the voice of a man between the banks of Ulai, and he called out and said, "Gabriel, give this man an understanding of the vision." So he came near to where I was standing, and when he came I was frightened and fell on my face; but he said to me, "Son of man, understand that the vision pertains to the time of the end."*

2. I Saw...
    Revelation 10:1, 3 – John the beloved on the Isle of Patmos – *And I saw another strong angel coming down out of heaven, clothed with a cloud; and the rainbow was upon his head, and his face was like the sun, and his feet like pillars of fire...and he cried out with a loud voice, as when a lion roars, and when he had cried out, the seven peals of thunder uttered their voices.*

3. I Felt...
    Zechariah 4:1 – *Then the angel who was speaking with me returned, and roused me as a man who is awakened from his sleep.*

    Acts 12:21-23 – *And on an appointed day Herod, having put on his royal apparel, took his seat on the rostrum and began delivering an address to them. And the people kept crying out, "The voice of a god and not of a man!" And immediately an angel of the Lord struck him because he did not give God the glory, and he was eaten by worms and died.*

4. In a Dream...
    Matthew 1:19-21 – *And Joseph her husband, being a righteous man, and not wanting to disgrace her, desired to put her away secretly. But when he had considered this, behold an angel of the Lord appeared to him in a dream saying, "Joseph, son of David, do not be afraid to take Mary as your wife; for that which has been conceived in her is of the Holy Spirit."*

5. In a Vision...
    Acts 10: 3, 4 – *About the ninth hour of the day he clearly saw in a vision an angel of God who had just come in to him, and said to him, "Cornelius!" And fixing his gaze upon him and being much alarmed, he said, "What is it Lord?" And he said to him, "Your prayers and alms have ascended as a memorial before God."*

B. Discernment and Our Five Senses – Quoted from *The Seer* [20]
Discernment is a gift from God. This is true whether we are talking about general discernment between good and evil or discerning of spirits. Only in the rarest of cases does this gift come "full-blown" into a believer's life. For most of us, discernment grows over time as we nurture it carefully from day to day. More often than not, discernment operates through our five senses, and becomes strong in us through practice. Consider these words from the Book of Hebrews: *"But solid food is for the mature, who because of practice have their senses trained to discern good and evil"* (Hebrews 5:14).

Some things we learn by experience and some we learn by watching others. We learn discernment by practice. When we submit ourselves to the Lordship of Christ, He washes us clean from the defilement of the world, the flesh, and the demonic realm of the spirit. Our five natural senses—sight, smell, taste, touch, and hearing—are free then to be trained in the discernment of good and evil. The closer we walk with Christ, and the more we submit our mind and will to Him, the more acute our senses will become in discernment. It is a progressive unfolding.

One of the operative principles of the Kingdom of God that applies in every area of life is that our faithfulness in little things leads to our being entrusted with greater things. As we prove faithful with what God has given us, He will give us more. For example, our faithfulness in managing natural mammon will lead to our being given rule over what Jesus called true spiritual riches. It is a simple principle: faithfulness in the natural will bring increase in the realm of the spirit.

The more we yield our natural five senses to the Lord, the more the anointing of God can come upon them, making us progressively more sensitive to His promptings. The more we learn to recognize and obey those promptings, the more promptings we will receive. As we prove ourselves faithful with a little, the Lord will entrust us with more.

Basically, discernment is perception, which can come in a variety of ways. Sometimes it is as simple as an inner knowledge, a "gut feeling," that we cannot explain yet somehow know is real. This kind of spiritual perception is often so subtle that we can easily miss it or attribute it to something else, such as a "hunch."

Seeing is another avenue of perception. As we have already observed, seeing can be internal through images in the mind's eye, or external through an open vision. Sometimes it may be nothing more than a flash of light that brings a strong sense of a spiritual presence in the room, such as an angel. At other times, we may see an outline form or even a kind of fog of His glory filling the room. This again is a part of the "seer" package – divine perception. As our discernment grows, we may observe a kind of shimmering presence or, eventually, a fully defined vision, whether internal or external.

Sometimes spiritual discernment will come through our sense of smell. Many people have testified to sensing the presence of the Lord accompanied by the smell of roses. It is also possible at times to identify the enemy in the same way. A particular situation may not "smell right," even if we don't quite understand why. All we know is that it smells bad. There may be an actual unpleasant odor associated with the situation, such as the smell of rotten eggs. If there is no visible, apparent cause for the odor, it may be an indicator that an unclean spirit is present. Often, I have discerned addictions in a person's life through this means. I actually "smell" a type of smoke that comes from a particular form of addiction – I then know in part how to proceed in ministering in that situation.

What about spiritual perception through the sense of taste? Have you ever heard someone say, "I don't know for sure what's going on, but this just leaves a bad taste in my mouth"? That phrase may be literal or figurative. In Ezekiel 3:3, the prophet, during a vision, eats a scroll that represents the word of the Lord, and it is "sweet as honey" in his mouth. John records a similar experience in Revelation 10:9-10 where he eats a scroll containing God's judgments on the nations. Although the scroll tastes as sweet as honey in John's mouth, it makes his stomach bitter.

As far as the sense of touch is concerned, spiritual discernment may take the form of a tingling feeling, or even pain, particularly in situations where the Lord is revealing areas where He wants to release physical healing or deliverance. At times I receive physical pains in my heart showing me wounding that has occurred in another's life as a tool to "set the captives free." This feeling arena can also be used to distinguish what spirit is in operation behind a certain activity.

Perception through hearing is the realm most of us are probably most familiar with. At times there may be the sound of bells, the telephone ringing or even music. One of the most common sounds associated with spiritual perception is the sound of wind, such as occurred on the Day of Pentecost. One time, in the middle of the night, a supernatural wind came blowing through a closed bedroom widow of our house. My wife, Michal Ann, and I were instantly awakened. Angels were released. Messages from God came our way. With the wind came His presence!

No matter which of our senses bring us spiritual perception, we are tapping into a grace gift of God. Consistency and growth in this area calls for us to have our hearts set toward the Lord Jesus Christ. All of our affections must be focused on Him. And He will grace or anoint our natural senses with the Holy Spirit to perceive even the Angels of God!

Reflection Questions
Lesson Nine: Discerning the Angelic Presence

Answers to these questions can be found in the back of the study guide.

Fill in the Blank

1. A gift of the Holy Spirit enables one to know the true _____ of the spiritual _____ behind an activity.

2. List the three main warnings concerning angelic beings:

   a. _____

   b. _____

   c. _____

3. The imperfect state of revelation is directly linked to the imperfect state of the _____ who deliver it – not to an imperfect _____!

4. What were five ways angels were experienced in the Bible?

   a. _____

   b. _____

   c. _____

   d. _____

   e. _____

True or False

5. Discerning of spirits also involves discerning of angels, because they are spiritual beings. _____

6. Evil and deceived false prophets are the major source of erroneous accounts to God's people today. _____

Continued on the next page.

Scripture Memorization

7. Write out and memorize I John 4:1-3.

8. Review the nine scriptural tests (Section III, D) we can apply to all spiritual activity that we receive to check for accuracy, authority, and validity. Consider one past "spiritual activity" that was from the Lord and one you discovered was not. For each one, write down which tests they passed and which they failed.

Lesson Ten:
Angelic Intervention through Intercession

I. A REVIEW OF ANGELIC ASSIGNMENTS

A. Three Primary Functions

1. Psalms 148:2, 5 – Praise and worship unto God.

2. Hebrews 1:7, 14 – Ministering spirits, flames of fire to render service to those who will inherit salvation.

3. Psalms 103:20, 21 – Angels excel in strength, obey the voice of His word, and perform God's Word.

B. Types of Activities

1. Minister the presence of the Lord
2. Messengers pronouncing God's will
3. Release understanding in dreams and visions
4. Help to give guidance and direction
5. Deliverance
6. Protection
7. Death of the saints
8. Release strength
9. Healing instruments
   (Types of Activities #10-15 are detailed in Lesson 12)
10. Praise and worship
11. Spiritual warfare
12. Bind demonic powers
13. Divine watchers
14. Reapers and gatherers
15. Execute God's judgments

II. FIVE FOUNDATIONAL PREMISES

A. Believers Are Co-Workers with Christ
God's resources are released by man's invitation of intercession.

B. God Hears and Answered Prayers
Prayer and intercession influences or helps determine the destiny of individuals and the direction of nations.

C. There Is an Innumerable Company of Angels Available

Heaven's army of angelic hosts is waiting for their next assignment and ready to be dispatched – (Unemployed Angels!)

Jeremiah 33:22 – *As the hosts of heaven cannot be counted and the sand of the sea cannot be measured.*

Hebrews 12:22 – *But you have come to Mount Zion and to the city of the living God, the heavenly Jerusalem, and to myriads of angels.*

D. Angels Are Involved in both the Spiritual and Practical Affairs of Mankind

Angels are released from God's throne in heaven into the affairs of man. They are involved in all facets of life in both the spiritual and in everyday normal activities of man.

E. Angels Are Used to Deliver God's Answers to Man's Prayers

Angels are especially utilized and involved in delivering the answers to our prayers from the throne of God.

III. THREE SCRIPTURAL EXAMPLES OF ANGELIC INTERVENTION THROUGH INTERCESSION

A. With Abraham and Lot – Lessons from Genesis 18 and 19

1. Genesis 18 – Prayerful example of Abraham's intercession for Sodom and Gomorrah.
2. Genesis 19: 1 – Two angels tell Lot's situation.
3. Genesis 19:11 – The ungodly men outside Lot's house are stricken with blindness.
4. Genesis 19:16 – Next, the angels lead Lot and his family out of the city before the destruction takes place. (This demonstrates the compassion of God.)
5. Genesis 19:20 – *Hurry, escape there, for I cannot do anything until...* This shows God's desire to deliver the righteous before the judgment occurred.
6. Genesis 19:29 – *God remembered Abraham.* (This is the key verse.) What did God remember? Abraham's intercession!

B. With Peter and the Church – Lessons from Acts 12:5-12

1. Acts 12:7-10 – Peter was kept in jail, an angel appeared to him. A light shone, woke Peter up, and the two chains which had held him fell off. He was told to "Gird thyself, and bind on thy sandals." He then passed by two guards, the iron gate to the prison opened, and he goes out into the street as angel departed.

2. Acts 12:11-12 – Next, Peter goes to the house of John Mark's mother where many had gathered to pray for him. A young woman named Rhoda came to door. She knew Peter's voice and went to tell the others, "You're crazy!" was their response. "No, it is his angel." Peter kept on knocking. They went to the door, and opening it, were amazed. It really was Peter! This caused such excitement that Peter had to admonish them to calm down and not be so noisy in their excitement to see him delivered out of the hand of Herod and those Jewish authorities who had sought to end his life.

    Peter told them to inform James and the other apostles that he was alright after all. When the matter became known to the wicked king, he demanded the lives of the jail keepers as punishment that they had somehow managed to allow Peter to escape.

3. Acts 12:5-12 – The emphasis is on verses 5 and 12. What was the church doing before the angel was released? Praying fervently! Thus we have another example of angelic intervention as a result of man's intercession.

C. With Daniel – Lessons from Daniel 9 and 10

1. Daniel 9:20-23 – *Now while I was speaking and praying, and confessing my sin and the sin of my people Israel, and presenting my supplication before the LORD my God in behalf of the holy mountain of my God, while I was still speaking in prayer, then the man Gabriel, whom I had seen in the vision previously, came to me in my extreme weariness about the time of the evening offering. He gave me instruction and talked with me and said, "O Daniel, I have now come forth to give you insight with understanding." At the beginning of your supplications the command was issued, and I have come to tell you, for you are highly esteemed; so give heed to the message and gain understanding of the vision."*

2. Daniel 10:12-14 – *Then he said to me, "Do not be afraid, Daniel, for from the first day that you set your heart on understanding this and on humbling yourself before your God, your words were heard, and I have come in response to your words. But the prince of the kingdom of Persia was withstanding me for twenty-one days; then behold, Michael, one of the chief princes, came to help me, for I had been left there with the kings of Persia. Now I have come to give you an understanding of what will happen to your people in the latter days, for the vision pertains to the days yet future."*

3. Daniel 10:20, 21 – *Then he said, "Do you understand why I came to you? But I shall now return to fight against the prince of Persia; so I am going forth, and behold, the prince of Greece is about to come. However, I will tell you what is inscribed in the writing of truth. Yet there is no one who stands firmly with me against these forces except Michael your prince."*

IV. THE RELATIONSHIP OF PRAYER, JUDGMENT AND MERCY

A. Revelation 8 and 16

1. Revelation 8:3-7

   a. First: Angels gather the praise and prayer of the saints (vs.4)
   b. Second: Goes into the censer with the fire on the on altar before God (vs. 2, 5).
   c. Third: It is thrown back down to earth. (Remember, what goes up, must come down!)

2. Why?

   a. Mercy triumphs over judgment.
   b. Pockets of mercy amidst the judgment of God.

3. Revelation 8:5 – Then voices, thundering, lightning, earthquakes, (signs and wonders) are released.

4. Revelation 8:6 – Then angels prepare to blow trumpets so that the righteous end-time judgments of God begin.

5. The supernatural activities in Revelation 16 are inter-related to those found in Revelation 8.

B. Zephaniah 2:1-3

Gather yourselves together, yes, gather, nation without shame,
Before the decree takes effect--
The day passes like the chaff--
Before the burning anger of the LORD comes upon you,
Before the day of the LORD'S anger comes upon you.
Seek the LORD,
All you humble of the earth
Who have carried out His ordinances?
Seek righteousness, seek humility.
Perhaps you will be hidden
In the day of the LORD'S anger.

The prophet Zephaniah again gives us the principle that the Lord gives time for His people to gather themselves together and call on His Name before His judgments, anger or ordinances are released. His desire is that we be hidden in such a day.

C. A Vivid Dream While in Jerusalem

On the Day of Atonement in 2005, I was given a series a detailed dreams while in Jerusalem, Israel. In one of these dreams, I was shown three angels each holding a shofar or a ram's horn.

The first angel stood in rapt attention and had already blown its trumpet. When the sound of the horn went forth, the word "calamity" was released. The word "natural disasters" appeared in the dream indicating the increase of hurricanes, volcanic eruptions, earthquakes, and such phenomena. Next in the dream, I saw a second angel step forward and put a shofar to its mouth to blow. Out came a sound declaring "plagues" were being released. This appeared to be a pronouncement that was happening right at that moment.

A third angel was standing behind observing what was transpiring. This angel had not yet been commissioned to release its sound. I was not told what the pronouncement of this third angel would be. But I was keenly aware that there was yet time to intercede before the declaration took place.

D. Ezekiel 9:3-6

And the glory of the God of Israel was gone up from the cherub, whereupon he was, to the threshold of the house. And he called to the man clothed with linen, which had the writer's inkhorn by his side. And the Lord said unto him, "Go through the midst of the city, through the midst of Jerusalem, and set a mark upon the foreheads of the men that sigh and that cry for all the abominations that be done in the midst thereof." And to the others he said in mine hearing, "Go ye after him through the city, and smite: let not your eye spare, neither have ye pity: Slay utterly old and young, both maids, and little children, and women: but come not near any man upon whom is the mark; and begin at my sanctuary." Then they began at the ancient men which were before the house.

1.   The angel was told by God to mark the intercessors.

2.   What was the mark put upon the foreheads of the people? Some say the mark was the Hebrew letter Taw, the final letter of the Hebrew alphabet, which resembles an "X" or the cross of Christ. Jack Hayford comments from the Sprit-Filled Life Bible, which he edited, that this mark, placed by a seventh warrior angel "clothed with linen" (v. 3), was for protection (see Revelation 7:3) and symbolized that God would spare the righteous remnant.

3.   Who received this mark from the angel?
     All who sighed and groaned over the abominations of the city of Jerusalem were privileged to receive this sign of protection.

V.   CONCLUSION

Yes, it is true! Angelic intervention is released in response to man's intercession. It is time to intercede! Let heaven's angelic army be released into the affairs of man as a result of our invitation called prayer!

Reflection Questions
Lesson Ten: Angelic Intervention through Intercession

Answers to these questions can be found in the back of the study guide.

Fill in the Blank

1. Angelic intervention is released in response to our _____.

2. Prayer and intercession influences or helps determine the destiny of _____ and the direction of _____.

3. What goes _____, must come _____.

Multiple Choice – Choose the best answer from the list below:

A.	Hiding	C.	Angels
B.	Nature	D.	Praying

4. God often utilizes _____ to deliver the answers to our prayers.

5. Before the angel released Peter from prison, the church was _____.

True or False

6. There are a limited number of angels to respond to our intercession. _____

7. Angels are involved in *all* facets of life, including our everyday activities. _____

8. The Lord gives time for His people to gather themselves together and call on His Name before His judgments, anger or ordinances are released. _____

Continued on the next page.

Scripture Memorization

9. Write out and memorize Psalm 103:20-21.

10. What was the primary insight you received from this lesson?

Lesson Eleven:
Israel, the Harvest and the End Times

I. THE LATTER RAIN OF GOD'S SPIRIT

A. Joel 2:28, 29 – His Spirit upon All Flesh
It will come about after this that I will pour out My Spirit on all mankind; and your sons and daughters will prophesy, Your old men will dream dreams, Your young men will see visions. Even on the male and female servants I will pour out My Spirit in those days.

B. Hosea 6:1-3 – The Response to God's Rebuke
Come; let us return to the LORD. For He has torn us, but He will heal us; He has wounded us, but He will bandage us. He will revive us after two days; He will raise us up on the third day, that we may live before Him. So let us know, let us press on to know the LORD. His going forth is as certain as the dawn; And He will come to us like the rain, like the spring rain watering the earth.

C. Matthew 25: 1-13 – The Parable of the Ten Virgins
"Then the kingdom of heaven will be comparable to ten virgins, who took their lamps and went out to meet the bridegroom. Five of them were foolish, and five were prudent. For when the foolish took their lamps, they took no oil with them, but the prudent took oil in flasks along with their lamps. Now while the bridegroom was delaying, they all got drowsy and began to sleep. "But at midnight there was a shout, 'Behold, the bridegroom! Come out to meet him.' "Then all those virgins rose and trimmed their lamps. The foolish said to the prudent, 'Give us some of your oil, for our lamps are going out.' "But the prudent answered, 'No, there will not be enough for us and you too; go instead to the dealers and buy some for yourselves.' And while they were going away to make the purchase, the bridegroom came, and those who were ready went in with him to the wedding feast; and the door was shut. Later the other virgins also came, saying, 'Lord, lord, open up for us.' But he answered, 'Truly I say to you, I do not know you.' Be on the alert then, for you do not know the day or the hour."

D. Acts 2:1-4 – The Day of Pentecost
When the day of Pentecost had come, they were all together in one place. And suddenly there came from heaven a noise like a violent rushing wind, and it filled the whole house where they were sitting. And there appeared to them tongues as of fire distributing themselves, and they rested on each one of them. And they were all filled with the

Holy Spirit and began to speak with other tongues, as the Spirit was giving them utterance.

II. ANGELS AND THEIR ROLE WITH ISRAEL IN SCRIPTURE

Angels know the land of Israel better than you know your own neighborhood. We see angels throughout the history of the Jewish people, including their pre-Hebrew history contained in the pages of the Bible. We can claim this shared history too, because our Old Testament comes directly from the Hebrew Scriptures. The first mention of angels appears as early as Genesis 3, where angels were posted to guard the gates of the Garden. Then, through book after book, whether it's a prophetic message or a royal accounting of a military battle, we see angels everywhere. Angels and Israel are inseparable.

A.   Gideon and the Angel – Judges 6:6-7, 11-12

Now it came about when the sons of Israel cried to the Lord on account of Midian... then the angel of the Lord came and sat under the oak that was in Ophrah, which belonged to Joash the Abiezrite, as his son Gideon was beating out wheat in the wine press in order to save it from the Midianites. The angel of the Lord appeared to him and said to him, "The Lord is with you, O valiant warrior."

Angel or no angel, Gideon was not convinced. These were threatening times, and he was not a noted warrior. To be sure that this messenger was from God, he asked him to wait for him to prepare an offering.

So Gideon said to Him, "If now I have found favor in Your sight, then show me a sign that it is You who speak with me. Please do not depart from here, until I come back to You, and bring out my offering and lay it before You."

And He said, "I will remain until you return."

Then Gideon went in and prepared a young goat and unleavened bread from an ephah of flour; he put the meat in a basket and the broth in a pot, and brought them out to him under the oak and presented them.

The angel of God said to him, "Take the meat and the unleavened bread and lay them on this rock, and pour out the broth." And he did so. Then the angel of the Lord put out the end of the staff that was in his hand and touched the meat and the unleavened bread; and fire sprang up from the rock and consumed the meat and the unleavened bread. Then the angel of the Lord vanished from his sight.

When Gideon saw that he was the angel of the Lord, he said, "Alas, O Lord God! For now I have seen the angel of the Lord face to face" (Judges 6:17-22).

God heard the Israelites' cry for help, and he sent an angel to notify a leader and help him muster the necessary troops, then he helped him go to battle and win.

B. Abraham and the Angels

1. Angel Declares Isaac's Birth
   An angelic delegation visited Abraham and Sarah by the oaks of Mamre. "Three men," who are assumed to have been angels, arrived and spoke to Abraham. He welcomed them hospitably, and soon he discovered that they were no ordinary travelers. The spokesman declared, with the authority of God Himself, "I will surely return to you at this time next year; and behold, Sarah your wife will have a son" (Gen. 18:10). Then he seemed to read Sarah's thoughts and he said, "Why did Sarah laugh, saying, 'Shall I indeed bear a child, when I am so old?' Is anything too difficult for the Lord? At the appointed time I will return to you, at this time next year, and Sarah will have a son." (Gen. 18:13-14)

2. Angel Visits Hagar – Genesis 16:7-11
   Now the angel of the Lord found her by a spring of water in the wilderness, by the spring on the way to Shur. He said, "Hagar, Sarai's maid, where have you come from and where are you going?"

   And she said, "I am fleeing from the presence of my mistress Sarai."

   Then the angel of the Lord said to her, "Return to your mistress, and submit yourself to her authority." Moreover, the angel of the Lord said to her, "I will greatly multiply your descendants so that they will be too many to count."

The angel of the Lord said to her further, "Behold, you are with child, and you will bear a son; and you shall call his name Ishmael, because the Lord has given heed to your affliction. He will be a wild donkey of a man, his hand will be against everyone, and everyone's hand will be against him; and he will live to the east of all his brothers."

3.   Angel Cares for Hagar and Ishmael – Genesis 14b-19
She departed and wandered about in the wilderness of Beersheba. When the water in the skin was used up, she left the boy under one of the bushes. Then she went and sat down opposite him, about a bowshot away, for she said, "Do not let me see the boy die." And she sat opposite him, and lifted up her voice and wept.

God heard the lad crying; and the angel of God called to Hagar from heaven and said to her, "What is the matter with you, Hagar? Do not fear, for God has heard the voice of the lad where he is. Arise, lift up the lad, and hold him by the hand, for I will make a great nation of him."

Then God opened her eyes and she saw a well of water; and she went and filled the skin with water and gave the lad a drink.

4.   Angel Provides for Abraham and Isaac – Genesis 22:9-12
Then they came to the place of which God had told him; and Abraham built the altar there and arranged the wood, and bound his son Isaac and laid him on the altar, on top of the wood.

Angels guided and preserved Abraham and his family over and over again. God wanted to achieve His plan to establish His chosen people, the Jews. He also wanted to establish and bless the other people groups who arose from Abraham's seed.

God's promises to the offspring of the patriarch Abraham, uttered through his angels, remain valid, even though, by and large, the people of the Middle East have to this day failed to realize how much of the promise is fulfilled in Yeshua, the Lord Jesus. The Jews don't believe that He's the Messiah they have been waiting for, and the Arab world doesn't realize that they even need a Savior.

That fact should compel us to our knees again and again. Jesus said, "I have other sheep, which are not of this fold; I must bring them also, and they will hear My voice; and they will become one flock with one shepherd" (John 10:16). We who have ourselves been "grafted in" to the vine of Israel (see Romans 11) can ask God to command his angels to break through the darkness all over the Middle East.

C. Daniel with the Archangel

1. Daniel 10:2-6
In those days, I, Daniel, had been mourning for three entire weeks. I did not eat any tasty food, nor did meat or wine enter my mouth, nor did I use any ointment at all until the entire three weeks were completed.

   On the twenty-fourth day of the first month, while I was by the bank of the great river, that is, the Tigris, I lifted my eyes and looked, and behold, there was a certain man dressed in linen, whose waist was girded with a belt of pure gold of Uphaz. His body also was like beryl, his face had the appearance of lightning; his eyes were like flaming torches, his arms and feet like the gleam of polished bronze, and the sound of his words like the sound of a tumult.

2. Daniel 10:8-11
This angel, as we have seen in many other instances, caused great fear. The men who were with Daniel fled, even though they couldn't see the angel or hear his words, and Daniel himself was overcome:

   So I was left alone and saw this great vision; yet no strength was left in me, for my natural color turned to a deathly pallor, and I retained no strength. But I heard the sound of his words; and as soon as I heard the sound of his words, I fell into a deep sleep on my face, with my face to the ground.

   Then behold, a hand touched me and set me trembling on my hands and knees. He said to me, "O Daniel, man of high esteem, understand the words that I am about to tell you and stand upright, for I have now been sent to you." And when he had spoken this word to me, I stood up trembling.

   The angel proceeded to explain what was happening and what was going to happen, and in order to do so, he had to make it possible for Daniel to withstand his powerful presence.

3.   Daniel 10:12b-19

I have come in response to your words. But the prince of the kingdom of Persia was withstanding me for twenty-one days; then behold; Michael, one of the chief princes, came to help me, for I had been left there with the kings of Persia.

"Now I have come to give you an understanding of what will happen to your people in the latter days, for the vision pertains to the days yet future."

When he had spoken to me according to these words, I turned my face toward the ground and became speechless. And behold, one who resembled a human being was touching my lips; then I opened my mouth and spoke and said to him who was standing before me, "O my lord, as a result of the vision anguish has come upon me, and I have retained no strength. For how can such a servant of my lord talk with such as my lord? As for me, there remains just now no strength in me, nor has any breath been left in me."

Then this one with human appearance touched me again and strengthened me. He said, "O man of high esteem, do not be afraid. Peace be with you; take courage and be courageous!"

Now as soon as he spoke to me, I received strength and said, "May my lord speak, for you have strengthened me."

This angel was probably the archangel Gabriel, and he was explaining what the most superior of all archangels, Michael, was going to do. (Largely because of Daniel's account, the Jews since his time have claimed Michael as the guardian angel of Israel.)

4.   Daniel 10:20-21

Then he said, "Do you understand why I came to you? But I shall now return to fight against the prince of Persia; so I am going forth, and behold, the prince of Greece is about to come. However, I will tell you what is inscribed in the writing of truth. Yet there is no one who stands firmly with me against these forces except Michael your prince."

5.   Daniel 12:1 – The Time of the End

Now at that time Michael, the great prince who stands guard over the sons of your people, will arise. And there will be a time of distress such as never occurred since there was a nation until that time; and at that time your people, everyone who is found written in the book, will be rescued. Many of those who sleep in the dust of the ground will awake, these to everlasting life, but the others to disgrace and everlasting contempt. Those who have insight will shine brightly like the brightness of the expanse of heaven, and those who lead the many to righteousness, like the stars forever and ever. But as for you, Daniel, conceal these words and seal up the book until the end of time; many will go back and forth, and knowledge will increase.

III. MODERN-DAY ANGELIC ENCOUNTERS IN THE HOLY LAND

Angels have intervened—often openly—at every crucial juncture in the history of Israel. We have had a chance to see this first-hand, especially since the re-establishment in 1948 of the state of Israel. The Six-Day War in June of 1967 was swift and successful, adding the Gaza Strip, the Sinai Peninsula, the West Bank, and the Golan Heights to the territory that Israel had already reclaimed. Then came the Yom Kippur War.

A. Yom Kippur War
The Yom Kippur War of 1973 could have meant the end of Israel as a state. Egypt, Jordan, Iraq, and Syria joined forces to mount a surprise attack and, they hoped, annihilate the Jews. Lance Lambert, an English pastor and intercessor who has long been a friend of Israel, was in Jerusalem when the war broke out, and he includes an account of angelic intervention in his book, *Battle for Israel,* which is now out of print. First, some background:

People think of the 1967 Six-Day War as a miracle, but it was nothing compared with the Yom Kippur War. In the years that lie ahead, when the whole truth comes out, we shall see that it was beyond all reason that Israel was not annihilated.

A few weeks after the war, I heard Golda Meir [the prime minister of Israel] say, "For the first time in our twenty-five year history, we thought we might have lost." Before then I had never heard a prominent Israeli so much as imply the possibility of defeat or admit to fear. At one point in the war, only ninety battered Israeli tanks stood between the powerful Egyptian army and Tel Aviv, yet Israel was not beaten....

In the Yom Kippur War, which was the first wholly technological war in Middle East history, approximately 4,000 tanks, 900 missile batteries, and even unproved new weapons were thrown into action. Egypt attacked with 3,000 tanks, 2,000 heavy guns, 1,000 aircraft, and 600,000 men.

The regular Israeli garrisons numbered only a few hundred men against the massive tank attack. With their greater numbers, the Egyptians should have been in El Arish if not in Gaza and Beersheba, within twenty-four hours and then the whole of Israel's heartland would have been exposed. There was nothing to stop them....

Egypt and Syria should have beaten Israel, but they were inexplicably prevented.... If they had swept on, the whole of central Israel would have been at their mercy. One Egyptian tank commander said later, "I was only half an hour's drive from the Mitla Pass, and there was nothing to stop me." Yet the fact is he stopped.

Likewise the Syrians should have been in Tiberias on the evening of the first day of the war but they too stopped.... Wave after wave of tanks bore down on [the Israeli Golani brigade]. Then when they came to within one mile of the headquarters, they halted. "'They saw the Lake of Galilee," he said, "they liked the view, and they stopped."[21]

In Lance's account, now we begin to see the hand of God, quite literally:

[An] Israeli captain without any religious beliefs said that at the height of the fighting on the Golan, he looked up into the sky and saw a great, grey hand pressing downwards as if it were holding something back. In my opinion that describes exactly what happened; without the intervention of God, Israel would have been doomed....

The fighting became increasingly severe. Galilee was shelled and the Syrians even used Frog missiles. There were many air raids in the north but then Syria was gradually pushed back. Meanwhile, Egypt was held in the Sinai where the greatest tank battle in world history was fought on Friday, October 19th. Much of the fighting was at such close range that they weren't even able to maneuver the tanks. Jordanian radio described it as 'Hell on earth'.[22]

Then the prayers began to go up, although not without a struggle:

Many of the Christians in Jerusalem felt that the main purpose of my being delayed there was for prayer.... [The warden of the Garden Tomb of Jesus offered us accommodation in a house there.] It was as if one was at the heart of things. Here was the natural centre for most of the Christians in Jerusalem.... I found here as everywhere else, that [genuine corporate prayer] is a lost art....

I was appalled that when Israel was in such great need, even Christian workers and servants of the Lord who had been clearly put there by God and really felt God calling them to pray for all that was going on at the time, were unable to pray together in depth.... So we held a school of prayer at the height of the war. Our burden was for the dying and wounded, Arab and Jew alike, that they might be saved; for the Israeli people, that the war might be used to turn them to God; for the invaders, that the Lord would paralyze and confuse them and especially for Jordan, that she would not enter the war....[23]

Lance and his group of intercessors saw their prayers answered, and it didn't take very long. Their fervent prayers included prayers for world leaders, who were deciding whether and how to become involved on both sides of the war. Some Christians, who had been tutored by the late Rees Howells in crisis intercession, felt that the enemy was trying to precipitate Armageddon. Prayer was not just a good idea; it was *vital*. Lance continues:

[Israel's] right to exist and her claim to destiny have always been contested. From the very beginning of her history the powers of darkness and evil have sought to destroy her from both without and within....

Israel represents spiritual realities and values. The Israel of old has left us with no great monuments such as the pyramids of ancient Egypt, or the great works of art such as the Chinese have left us. Instead she has given us the Word of God. In this we see her history set forth as a living, dynamic relationship with God. This lesson is seen both positively at the high points of her spiritual life and negatively during those times when she fell away from the Lord. God was teaching Israel that everything depends upon a right relationship to himself. It is in this way that the whole history of Israel is the setting forth of spiritual realities. It is not a matter of secular history but the unfolding of God's purpose to save mankind.[24]

Here's another testimony that I heard about what happened in the Yom Kippur War: "In the end, there were three thousand Egyptian tanks coming up from the Sinai, and the Egyptians heard an enormous, loud, roaring sound, and they stopped their progress." The Egyptians believed that it was the sound of hundreds of tanks coming against them. But there were not hundreds of Israeli tanks coming. The people who gave that testimony believed that God had released His angels, and that the roaring was the sound of it. Israel's troops heard the roaring sound too. Part of that battle did not occur. It was stopped in its tracks.

God did it in the time of Abraham. He did it in the time of Gideon. He did it in the time of Daniel. And He did it at the Yom Kippur War. Angels are on assignment, and they will be released in response to the fervent cries of God's people.

IV. TIMES OF THE HARVEST

A. Revelation 14:14-19 – Angels Are Involved in the Harvest
Then I looked, and behold, a white cloud, and sitting on the cloud was one like a son of man, having a golden crown on His head and a sharp sickle in His hand. And another angel came out of the temple, crying out with a loud voice to Him who sat on the cloud, "Put in your sickle and reap, for the hour to reap has come, because the harvest of the earth is ripe."

Then He who sat on the cloud swung His sickle over the earth, and the earth was reaped.

And another angel came out of the temple which is in heaven, and he also had a sharp sickle. Then another angel, the one who has power over fire, came out from the altar; and he called with a loud voice to him who had the sharp sickle, saying, "Put in your sharp sickle and gather the clusters from the vine of the earth, because her grapes are ripe."

So the angel swung his sickle to the earth and gathered the clusters from the vine of the earth, and threw them into the great wine press of the wrath of God.

In the fall of 2005, I started seeing in spiritual visions a company of angels descending into the earth realm that I had never seen before in my lifetime. I asked the Lord who they were. The word came to me, "These are my Harvest Angels. I have been waiting to send them."
- James W. Goll

I believe that these are the same category of angels that other prophets and seers have also been seeing and declaring their appearing.

B. Matthew 13:36-43 – The Reapers Are Angels
Then He left the crowds and went into the house. And His disciples came to Him and said, "Explain to us the parable of the tares of the field." And He said, "The one who sows the good seed is the Son of Man, and the field is the world; and as for the good seed, these are the sons of the kingdom; and the tares are the sons of the evil one; and the enemy who sowed them is the devil, and the harvest is the end of the

*age; and **the reapers are angels**. So, just as the tares are gathered up and burned with fire, so shall it be at the end of the age. The Son of Man will send forth His angels, and they will gather out of His kingdom all stumbling blocks, and those who commit lawlessness, and will throw them into the furnace of fire; in that place there will be weeping and gnashing of teeth. Then THE RIGHTEOUS WILL SHINE FORTH AS THE SUN in the kingdom of their Father. He, who has ears, let him hear."*

C.   Breakthrough Revival from Paul Keith Davis [25]

The angel stated that his name is "Breakthrough" and he has been assigned to the United States. That is what was articulated to Bob Jones in one of the most significant visitations he has ever received.

Over the past 12 years I have watched the revelatory realm open to Bob in profound ways. It was quite astounding for him to tell me that he has recently had the second most powerful visitation of his life. The only one higher came directly from the Lord Jesus Himself.

On Friday, March 24th, as Bob was preparing for prayer, he immediately went into an Acts 10:10 type of trance. Bob's highest revelations come in this way. As the visitation commenced, Bob saw what appeared to be 12 ordinary "men" approaching him. Although they had the appearance of men he knew they were angels. The one in front seemed to be the most prominent and served as spokesman for the group.

He said, "My name is 'Breakthrough' and I have now been assigned to the United States." For approximately 30 minutes the angel shared with Bob historical accounts of past revivals that transpired to God's glory that he was involved in. His job is to release breakthrough and awakening to initiate a wave of harvest by extracting all obstacles to God's plans while the other angels gather the harvest.

Most prominently, he shared his involvement in the life of Benson Idahosa. The angel specifically articulated that he has now been assigned to the United States from Nigeria. He had previously been intimately involved in the ministry of this great man of God throughout Nigeria and other African nations.

Without Bob knowing the natural history beforehand, the angel shared with him great revivals that brought many souls into God's Kingdom that he was responsible for. The angel specifically stated that he has been in the United States for approximately two years laying the groundwork for the next revival. A revival, he said, that present stadiums are not adequate to hold once it is fully manifested.

This revelation is particularly significant for me as it directly relates to a word that we have been sharing throughout the Body of Christ since October 2003.

Angels that Gather

In the fall of 2003, Wanda and I had been invited to participate in a dedication service with our friends at Vineyard Christian Fellowship in Albany, Oregon. This wonderful flourishing church had expanded its facility to a 1500 seat auditorium. Many of our ministry friends had accepted the invitation to participate in its dedication. Because of a prior commitment on the East Coast during this October week, we were not able to participate in the inaugural service beginning on Thursday.

On Friday October 17, Wanda and I arrived early at the airport to make the journey across the nation to Albany to join our friends Bob Jones, Bobby Connor, Don and Christine Potter and others who already involved in the services. The entirety of that day was spent on airplanes and in airports. It was not a positive spiritual atmosphere. The events of that day certainly did not prepare me for what transpired the moment I stepped into the sanctuary on that Friday evening.

Very often we have mistaken notion that we must spend extended periods of time in prayer and fasting for the Lord to speak to us in clear and concise ways. Naturally, that is a good way to position ourselves before God's Throne to hear from Him.

Nevertheless, the Lord also chooses to speak in ways that sometimes surprises us. The hardship of simple life issues on the island of Patmos surely made John's revelations all the more meaningful.

Clearly John's revelations are some of the most profound ever entrusted to man, but the principle is the same. The Lord will often speak to us in the midst of a storm, while in a great trial or even after a long day of airline travel.

A Shocking Revelation

Because of the length of time it required for us to make the trip, the service had already begun by the time we arrived. Don Potter was leading worship and the people were fully engaged in the service.
As our as escort opened the side door leading to the sanctuary I placed my first step into the new auditorium. Instantly, with that first

step, I was seeing both the natural and spiritual realms at the same time. Although my natural eyes were still seeing the people as they worshiped, my spiritual eyes were open to see the Spirit's realm. I clearly saw, with open eyes, angels standing from one corner of the building across the back to the other corner.

Each angel appeared to be about six to seven feet tall. They were standing approximately six feet apart and they each wore a white robe that reached to their feet. They were each watching the podium as Don Potter was leading worship. Some had golden belts that seemed to be made of a rope-like material and others had golden sashes of the exact same color that draped across their chest.

Their countenance was compassionate and caring. Some from heaven's host are fierce and overwhelming in appearance, but these seemed tender and loving. I initially struggled to find the right words to depict their demeanor.

End-Time Provision

My first question was, "who are they." The answer came immediately and emphatically. The Spirit said, "They are angels that gather." To my knowledge, I had never before heard that expression. "Angels that gather" was a fresh revelation to me.

As I took the seat next to the pastor I advised him that there were angels standing across the back of his Church. He asked what kind of angels and I firmly and authoritatively stated, "They are angels that gather," although that phrase was made known to me only moments before.

I needed a scripture to confirm my statement to the pastor. I fortunately was able to discover the biblical affirmation of this reality in Matthew 13.

Matthew 13:37-43 directly affects the latter day generation and outlines our provision for the end-time confrontation. Jesus said so in this passage. It is a clear outline of the spiritual conflict that will exist in the days immediately preceding His return.

In Matthew 13 the Lord gives the following interpretation involving the latter-day generation saying,

> *"And He said, 'The one who sows the good seed is the Son of Man, and the field is the world; and as for the good seed, these are the sons of the kingdom; and the tares are the sons of the evil one;*

and the enemy who sowed them is the devil, and the harvest is the end of the age; and the reapers are angels. "So just as the tares are gathered up and burned with fire, so shall it be at the end of the age.

'The Son of Man will send forth His angels, and they will gather out of His kingdom all stumbling blocks, and those who commit lawlessness, and will throw them into the furnace of fire; in that place there will be weeping and gnashing of teeth. Then THE RIGHTEOUS WILL SHINE FORTH AS THE SUN in the kingdom of their Father. He who has ears, let him hear.'" Matthew 13:37-43

The Bible plainly articulates that the field in which the Lord has sown good seed is the world. The one who sows the good seed is the Son of Man. The seed that He imparts are the children of the Kingdom. The Lord Jesus Himself clearly states that there are a host of angels designated for the end-time generation who will work collectively with God's people in the labor of the last-day harvest.

"Angels that gather" will not only collect the wheat into the barn but also extract stumbling blocks that interfere with the flourishing of God's Kingdom. This is the spiritual provision Bob was seeing in his experience. The main angel provided breakthrough while the others gathered the harvest.

Bob's Vision Continued

The angel called "Breakthrough" continued to speak with Bob about God's end-time strategy. He shared how Benson Idahosa was often commissioned into a nation or region with God's mandate. No matter what the opposition was, all obstacles were removed through "Breakthrough" so that a harvest of souls could be achieved. That is the model for these coming days and our promised harvest.

The angel then told Bob that everything he was observing in this vision was a prophecy. He then asked, "What do you see." Bob replied that their appearance seemed so ordinary. The angel's response was "precisely." "We are going to work with ordinary people who have fully yielded their spirit, soul and body to the Lord," he said.

Those used most prominently in this installment of God's plan will not boast in their wisdom or might, but in knowing the Lord intimately. Jeremiah 9:23-24 speaks of this attribute saying,

Let not a wise man boast of his wisdom, and let not the mighty man boast of his might, let not a rich man boast of his riches; but let him who boasts boast of this, that he understands and knows me, that I am the LORD who exercises loving kindness, justice and righteousness on earth; for I delight in these things," declares the LORD.

It is the Lord's intent during this season to fully mobilize the Body of Christ into its function as God's intermediary on the Earth. The foremost responsibility of the five-fold ministry is to equip God's people to do the work of the ministry. Even the feeblest among us should be as noble and victorious as the great worshiping-warrior, King David. (Zechariah 12:8)

Move, Move, Move

"Breakthrough" then shouted, "Move, move, move!" From this Bob knew that there would be at least three major expressions of this spiritual dynamic soon to take place. It also articulated our directive to move in faith on the earth in order to cooperate in the Spirit with this Heavenly host. This is an end-time strategy that is to be employed now.

The predominant Scripture to be utilized in this commissioning is Matthew 10:7-8 declaring,

"And as you go, preach, saying, 'The kingdom of heaven is at hand.' Heal the sick, raise the dead, cleanse the lepers, cast out demons. Freely you received, freely give."

This will be a season of harvest; a harvest of souls and a harvest of promises. Even so, it will come not by the mere articulation of words but also with power. That is the pattern of the early Church and the one we see demonstrated in the life and ministry of Benson Idahosa.

In Exodus 23, God promised to send an Angel before Israel to overcome every enemy and establish them in the land of promise. Their obedience to the Word assured their victory and released the Lord to remove sickness from their midst. In like fashion, a wave of healing will accompany this season of grace we are now entering.

Knowing the Timing

The presence of these angels will be very similar to the spiritual sign given to King David in his battle with the Philistines in II Samuel 5. When David inquired of the Lord for divine strategy and precise timing, the Lord released "breakthrough" to route all opposition to grant a complete victory! The scripture emphasizes that,

> *David came to Baal-perazim, and defeated them there; and he said, "The LORD has broken through my enemies before me like the breakthrough of waters." Therefore he named that place Baal-perazim. (The master of breakthrough)*

Victory is achieved in the spirit realm first, and then manifested in the natural realm. In the continuation of this prophetic scenario, the Bible tells us David knew to move against his enemies when he discerned wind blowing among the balsam trees.

Following that example, we will learn in this day to co-operate with the Lord's timing when we discern God's winds, His angels, moving on our behalf. There will be cooperation between heaven and earth in this powerful dynamic. (Hebrews 1:7)

Finally, when the angel asked again what Bob saw, the only other dynamic in the vision that Bob could perceive seemed to be the angel's friendly demeanor. That in itself is also a prophecy. The end-time Church will learn to cooperate fully with the spiritual host assigned to us as friends learn to cohesively work in unison with their closest friends.

It is our responsibility y to meticulously follow the Holy Spirit's leadership to fully activate every spiritual dynamic and resource allotted to us. We release on the earth what we discern in the Spirit.

Judah's Twins

One final Scripture reference the angel gave to Bob Jones in his visitation came from Genesis 38:27-30. In this passage we discover the birthing of Judah's twins. The messenger emphasized the prophetic significance of the names given to these infants as a parabolic picture.

Perez = Breach; Zarach = dawning/rising

If we are to qualify to be utilized in this spiritual move we must possess boldness and determination. It would be a breach for us to put our hand to this task and then draw it back. According to Hebrew 10:37-39,

> *For yet a little while, and He who is coming will come and will not tarry. Now the just shall live by faith; but if anyone draws back, my soul has no pleasure in him. But we are not of those who draw back to perdition, but of those who believe to the saving of the soul.*

We cannot be among those who drawback because of opposition or fear, but rather among those who press forward to see breakthrough achieved.

A Confirming Visitation

As a final confirmation to this revelation, the Lord also visited with a friend of ours while in Nigeria in 2004 with the same revelation. At the time that I wrote our March 2004 newsletter outlining the vision of the "angels that gather, our friend, Pastor Randy Demain had accepted an invitation to participate in a missionary trip to Nigeria.
While in an open air meeting, Randy watched as the Holy Spirit accomplished virtually every manifestation we read about in the book of Acts. Mighty miracles, signs and wonders were taking place in this meeting. Many souls came into God's Kingdom through that demonstration of His Spirit.

That evening when Randy returned to his room he could not sleep because of excitement and decided to simply worship the Lord. As he did, he heard an audible voice ask, "I have a gift for you will you receive it?"

Much to his surprise it was the Lord asking if he would be willing to accept a spiritual gift. When he responded with an affirmation, Randy perceived with his open eyes the angel that the Lord desired to assign to him. His name was "Breakthrough Revival."

The Lord went on to explain to Randy that this angel had been assigned to Benson Idahosa until his death in 1998. The Lord shared how "Breakthrough" removes all obstacles and stumbling blocks so that God's people can pray to the Lord of the Harvest and reap a bountiful gathering of souls.

This was explained to Randy in the visitation before he returned home and actually read our newsletter outlining this exact end-time strategy. For the past two years Randy and I have been sharing this revelation laying the groundwork for a wave of harvest. We believe this will be a harvest of harvesters.

By Paul Keith Davis – www.whitedoveministries.org

D. From Shawn Bolz – A Dream on May 18, 2006 "The Process of Personal Breakthrough"

I was in a deep sleep – unaware that outside of my dreams, there was a raging storm here in Alabama. Lightning split the sky at a rate that my west coast eyes were not used to, and I believe it was used to affect my dream.

In this night dream, I saw a flash of light and a man appeared in the light; it was an angel from Heaven with the appearance of a strong man. He appeared next to a human male, who was waiting for Heaven to respond wholeheartedly.

Another flash came and there appeared two praying men and four angels. The next flash came and there were two men, a woman, two children, and twelve angels. Then flashes came so rapidly, with people and angels appearing and multiplying, that I could not keep up with the numbers. All I knew was: The light of Heaven was actively shooting towards the earth and divine placement was happening.

I awoke from the outside lightning storm, knowing I had just witnessed the emerging generation of revivalists – receiving divine helpers from Heaven--assigned to them for personal breakthrough, so they could help break a generation into the fullness of God.

The Revivalists Are Coming!

Although the term revival is often overused and exaggerated in emphasis, there is a generation of revivalists coming up out of the wilderness right now. These revivalists will not be the stereotypical, hyper-charismatic personalities, just known for preaching a fiery message to stir up the masses. These revivalists will be empowered to bring individuals, regions, countries, continents and the world, into a true conversion experience, to look like what God desired from the beginning: A full manifestation of His nature on the earth through the ones He loves--us.

When I was praying about this generation, I saw a process of personal breakthrough, which starts with a spiritual awakening to the Kingdom of God. This causes a desperate hunger (that we might decrease, so that He can increase), a hunger for the fruit of Heaven to come. Then there is a preparation like in Hebrews 12, preparing us to touch the mountain of God (Hebrews 12:22).

Then the Lord comes with an impartation that installs the nature of Christ (II Peter 1:4) into us. Lastly, there is a manifestation of Christ through us to the world, by which He is seen in us to bring:

1. Awakening.
2. Desperation.
3. Preparation.
4. Installation.
5. Manifestation.

I believe there are those who have been in this process and are about to receive their breakthrough in an unprecedented way, which will cause an awakening all over the world.

True revival is sustained by the lives that are constantly transforming into the image of Christ

If you remove this element of the Holy Spirit changing and transforming us, then you remove the power of the revival. If you want breakthrough, then you are asking for this kind of process. If you go through this process, you are going to go through radical transformation and change.

When Bob Jones and Paul Keith released the word about the angel named "Breakthrough," I felt a very strange momentum come upon me. I felt very aware that the breakthrough these angels have come to help us with, has never been opened this way before.

I began to ask myself, "Is this what the men who first broke the sound barrier felt, when they were up in the sky?" What if we are going to break the barrier of the spirit realm? What if we are breaking through into Heaven in such a real way, that the heavy glory comes upon us like generations have dreamed about and prayed about? Some generation is going to do it--break into the end-time anointing, why not us?

The Scroll with Wings

As I have been anticipating breakthrough, I have been pondering steps we may need to take in order for this to come. I was praying and began to think of the repentance we may need to do here geographically--and the strong men that have yet to be broken. As I was interceding, I saw again a vision I had in February, of a scroll flying towards me. It had large graceful wings that were white and when it got close, it had the scripture Romans 9:16 written upon it:

> *"It does not therefore depend on man's desire or effort, but on God's mercy."*

We are in a season of standing on this word--that His mercy, not our effort, will make a way for His desire. I believe this truth revealed can help many who feel they need to work for what Jesus has already paid the price for...

Breakthrough is coming – because it's on Heaven's timetable to come right now.

By Shawn Bolz – www.whitedoveministries.org

E. Angels in Bennington, Vermont [26]

On Wednesday March 14, 2006 Oscar Caraballo (a pastor from Bennington, VT) was beginning to experience something very profound in the Lord. He says as he was walking into the Vermont School of Prayer Conference in Burlington VT at 7:45 pm something was taking place.

"I didn't walk into a normal place, the atmosphere was transformed into a cozy place of rest, the Spirit of the Lord was intense during the meeting." A little while later the Spirit of the Lord began to whisper in His ear about the Glory of the Lord being released in the Northeastern United States. "After some time soaking in the Spirit of the Lord, the Holy Spirit whispered in my ear, 'Do you want to see the intensity of the situation outside of this peaceful place?' I responded, 'Yes.'

"Immediately the Holy Spirit lifted me up to the top of the building, I noticed that it was surrounded by a structure of white pearl stones, and on each of the four corners of this structure there was an Angel in an anticipation mode. He told me the protection of the Lord was in this place of worship.

"On Thursday March 15, 2006 as they were taking the offering the Lord said, "My protection is on this place and for every seed that goes in the ground today will come back one hundred times increase.

"After the offering Danny Steyne and others were standing in front of me worshiping the Lord. John Hamill said that some people had FIRE in their hands and they needed to pray for the person that was next to them. I prayed for Debbie Dougherty. Soon after that Danny was standing right in front of me, and an Angel was standing right next to him, this Angel turned and looked at me and threw a ball of fire at me and I was able to catch it in my right hand. The Angel then reached over and put his hand in the ball of FIRE and said to me, 'How much do you want this ball of FIRE?' and I replied, 'Very much.'

"The Angel then pulled me to the front of the church and he pushed me to my knees in front of Danny and in front of the entire congregation. The Angel then started to pull me side to side and moving me with a tremendous speed in a circular motion. Then he stopped pulling me and put me face down in the middle of the building.

"My hands were extended still holding the fire ball as I was on the floor! Then the Angel forcefully pulled the fire ball and took the ball of FIRE from my hands." John Hamill was sharing the word at that time and he was speaking about the FIRE of the Lord.

"The Angel made it clear that the ball of fire was not for me but for everyone in that place. Then another Angel came to me and said wait for further instructions from the Lord. Danny Steyne came up to me and said the Lord told him to tell me, 'You need to go!' The Angel came once again and said, 'Go to Bennington, Vermont now!' It was 11:00 PM by then and the drive to Bennington was 3 hours."

Three hours later Oscar arrived in Bennington. The Lord told him to go to the church building in the center of downtown Bennington and not go home. He opened the door and began to experience a phenomenal visitation of the Lord.

"I opened the door and to my surprise in the middle of the church were standing seven Angels of FIRE. To my right side was a Powerful Angel. He told me that his name is Gabriel and he introduced me to the Angels of FIRE. He told me that these were the Lord's COVENANT ANGELS. He said that power is released when they combine and work together. One of the Angels came directly towards me and he said 'I am the one who make things happen, there is no mountain that will stop you from going to bring the Word of God to those who need Jesus with them.' They carried the colors of the rainbow always standing from right to left. Violet, Indigo, Blue, Green, Yellow, Orange, Red ...In that order...But they all work together. There is nothing they cannot do by the power of the Lord. They are making things happen. The Angel said once again, I AM the one who make things happen, I will go through anything that is in your way."

Each angel represented a facet of the workings of God. Each moved with unprecedented power in each of their specific callings, but when they worked together and combined their giftings, nothing stood in their way.

"Each of these Angels were very innocent looking, but very powerful. They were also the most loving angels I have ever encountered. They helped you fall in love with God more and more! They had so much love in them!

"Then the Angel took my hand and led me to the outside of the church building and lifted me up in the air and showed me Mount Snow and the mountains around New England. At the top of the Mountains it was something that looks like a chariot or train of FIRE running on top of the mountains. One of the Angels said to me, 'The chariots of FIRE move throughout mountains of New England.' Then 'The Angel that makes things happen' said to me. 'We will show you more.' Then they lifted me up just one inch more but it felt like a thousand feet more. He pointed with his left hand and with his right hand he was worshiping the Lord in Heaven. Behind the mountains I saw the largest army of Angels that I could have ever imagined, the Angel said that 365 legions of ANGELS ARE READY TO INVADE NEW ENGLAND!" The mountain I was looking directly at was Mount Snow."

He said, "This is the Supernatural invading the Natural, and it is going to happen soon! He then said, "Come through the gate, this is the Lord doing this, you will come through the gate, not over the fence to steal like a thief. This move will be public, and not hidden!' He told me that already there have been Special Forces that have been sent under the barbed wire in New England. These are the men and women who continue to go into New England with the Revival Fire message. He then said, "Revival has infiltrated behind enemy lines!'"

V.   THE END TIMES CHURCH

A.   Embracing our Opportunity – Seizing the Moment

An angel of the Lord appeared to me in Buenos Aires, Argentina, and declared, "Seize the Moment!" So I echo that heavenly word and declare that the Lord's appointed *kairos* moment has come. We have arrived at a "fullness of time" juncture of church history. God's end-time plan is being sent in motion.

What is our role? Our role is to continue to pursue the simplicity and purity of devotion to Christ Jesus and become men and women of prayer. This empowers the spiritual host to battle on our behalf in the spiritual realm to achieve notable victories to the Lord's glory.

There is a spiritual principle that states where evil abounds, grace does much more abound. The Lord is extending an incredible opportunity for His great-grace to be manifested. We must embrace every divine opportunity and employ these incredible gifts being delegated to us at this crucial moment. Embrace the opportunity.

Let's welcome the heavenly army into the earth realm. Let's lift our prayers and petitions for His plans, purposes and destiny to come forth in its fullness. Kingdom come! His will be done in our lives, families, and spheres of influence.

Yes, we welcome the messenger angels to come and release God's Word. We welcome the healing angels in Jesus Name to do their work. Those angels of the harvest that gather – we say, "Come!" Angels of your presence – oh how we need your assistance! So we cry, "Release the secret weapons – your angelic hosts – in Jesus' great Name and for His sake!"

B.   Hebrews 12:18-24

"For you have not come to a mountain that can be touched and to a blazing fire, and to darkness and gloom and whirlwind, and to the blast of a trumpet and the sound of words which sound was such that those who heard begged that no further word be spoken to them. For they could not bear the command, "IF EVEN A BEAST TOUCHES THE MOUNTAIN, IT WILL BE STONED." And so terrible was the sight, that Moses said, "I AM FULL OF FEAR and trembling." But you have come to Mount Zion and to the city of the living God, the heavenly Jerusalem, and to myriads of angels, to the general assembly and church of the firstborn who are enrolled in heaven, and to God, the Judge of all, and to the spirits of the righteous made perfect, and to Jesus, the mediator of a new covenant, and to the sprinkled blood, which speaks better than the blood of Abel."

So we join in with the heavenly choirs and we too cast down our crowns and declare, "Only He is worthy! Worthy is the Lamb of God, who was, who is and who is to come. Let all the earth be filled with His glory!" Amen and Amen!

Reflection Questions
Lesson Eleven: Israel, the Harvest and the End Times

Answers to these questions can be found in the back of the study guide.

Fill in the Blank

1. _____ and _____ are inseparable.

2. Those who have been _____ _____ to the vine of Israel can ask God to command his angels to break through the darkness all over the Middle East.

3. _____ and _____ should have beaten Israel in the Yom Kippur War, but they were _____ prevented."

Multiple Choice – Choose the best answer from the list below:

A.	Tells	C.	Sacrifice
B.	Stumbling blocks	D.	Empowers

4. Matthew 13 says that *"the Son of Man will send forth His angels, and they will gather out of His kingdom all _____."*

5. Being people of prayer devoted to Jesus _____ the spiritual host to battle on our behalf in the spiritual realm to achieve notable victories to the Lord's glory.

True or False

6. We see angels throughout the history of the Jewish people. _____

7. God's promises to the offspring of the patriarch Abraham, uttered through his angels, are no longer valid with the coming of Christ and the establishment of His Church. _____

8. Where evil abounds, grace does much more abound. _____

Continued on the next page.

Scripture Memorization

9. Write out and memorize Romans 9:16.

10. What was the primary insight you learned from this lesson

Lesson Twelve:
Angels and God's End Time Army

I.   MORE ASSIGNMENTS FOR THE ANGELS

A.   Review of Assignments of Angels

1.   Minister God's Presence
2.   Deliver God's Word or Message
3.   Release Dreams, Revelation and Understanding
4.   Guidance and Direction Given
5.   Deliverance Brought Forth
6.   Protection Granted
7.   Involved at the Death of the Saints
8.   Impart Strength
9.   Release Healing

B.   Praise and Worship

1.   Luke 2:14 – At Jesus birth, angels proclaimed praise to God.
2.   Revelation 5:11, 12 – Ten thousand times ten thousand angels declaring *"Worthy is the Lamb to receive..."*
3.   Genesis 32:1, 2 – This speaks of a special occasion where there was an encampment of God's angels.
4.   Events throughout Church history have been recorded where angelic praise is heard by man. Thus it was reported with Ern Baxter at a camp meeting in England.
5.   A conference in the 1990s in Kansas City at the Music Hall, where James saw angels blowing their horns and the praise went electric among the people.

I remember seeing angels with trumpets during a Passion for Jesus conference in Kansas City. We were in the Music Hall, which has a heart-shaped ceiling, in the midst of some radical worship. I looked up with my eyes open and I saw angels, and they were blowing horns. They would blow them repeatedly, and when they did, something was released from their trumpets that looked like honeybees were being sent forth, carrying something golden, which they took out over the people and dropped down on them. I think they were dropping the anointing on the people. I felt that apostolic mandates were being released. The atmosphere was absolutely *electric* with praise and worship. The angels joined with us and we joined with them. That night, it seemed that the angels were trumpeting and announcing and initiating something new, a new dimension of anointing and of God's glory.

C. Spiritual Warfare

1. Revelation 12:7 – Michael and his angels fought against the dragon and his angels in the original War in Heaven.
2. Daniel 10:13 – Michael fought and prevailed against the fallen angelic principality over Persia in response to Daniel's intercession.
3. Psalms 149:5-8 – The high praises of God are supernatural weapons of spiritual warfare to bind "their kings with chains, and their nobles with fetters of iron." Could these "kings" and "nobles" be fallen angelic rulers (Greek: archon) as well as lesser human rulers they manipulate?
4. Revelation 20:1-3 – An angel has a chain in this account. Who binds the forces of darkness? All three: God, man and the angels.

D. Divine Watchers

1. Daniel 4:13, 17 – Looking into the historical affairs of man.
2. Acts 12:20-23 – Looking, listening and responding.
3. I Timothy 5:21 – Have no partiality...

E. Pronounce and Execute God's Judgments

1. Genesis 19:11 – Blindness was released.
2. II Kings 19:3-5 – Assyrians struck.
3. Exodus 12:18-30 – Destroyer was sent out.
4. Acts 12:20-23 – Angel struck Herod and he died.
5. Revelation 16:17 – Trumpets and bowls are poured out by the angels releasing God's judgment in the earth.

F. Reapers and Gatherers

1. Revelation 14:6 – Gospel to preach.
2. Revelation 14:14-19 – Uses to reap the end time harvest.
3. Matthew 13:39-42 – To gather the lawless.
4. Matthew 24:31 – Gather the elect unto the Lord.

II.   STORIES FROM THE WAR CHEST

A.   Praying through the Bible Out Loud 7 Times

A friend named Kevin Nolker in Warrensburg, Missouri, was told by the Lord in the late 1980s that is he would read through the entire Bible out loud seven times, it would do something in the spiritual realm to release the Jews of the Soviet Union to be able to return to their homeland in Israel.

Kevin, a mail carrier by occupation, for months read the Word of God day and night until his mission was complete. His wife, Debbie, prayed and fasted for 40 days for Kevin to have strength to complete his task.

James Goll and Bob Jones then ministered together at a fall retreat and these two came and stood in the line. Bob Jones stated, because of the authority that rests upon this man and woman in prayer and fasting, I now have authority to release this message. "Communism will fall and the Jews from the Land of the North will return to Israel. Places and cities of refuge will be needed though to protect the Jewish people as these last days events unfold."

B.   Saint Petersburg and the 40/70 Prayer Window

James Goll and Cindy Jacobs of Generals International led a team to help open the 40/70 Prayer Window for the nation of Russia in 2001. When praying in Saint Petersburg, Russia, overlooking the Gulf of Finland, James had an open vision where he saw the waters part and thousands of Jewish people walking on dry land into safety. The Holy Spirit spoke to him that if the need be, that He would even supernaturally open the Gulf of Finland in the future so that the Jewish people could pass over into safety.

Then when in Moscow meeting with Messianic leaders from across the land of Russia, James began to speak. He shared the vision with these hungry Jewish leaders, it was confirmed that Cindy Jacobs had seen the same vision simultaneously of the Gulf of Finland parting.

God has many things in store in the future that will surely involve the work of angels as a part of God's End Time Army!

III. GOD'S END TIME ARMY [27]

(Portions reprinted from *The Watchmen Ministry*)

The following testimony comes from the life and ministry of the late Rolland Smith of Alpha and Omega Ministries, in St. Louis, Missouri. Rolland was a prophetic intercessor who traveled the globe with a team of men such as Kjell Sjoberg of Sweden and others in the 1980s. Jesus and His angels appeared to this humble intercessor and gave him direct orders.

"Jesus said that this prophetic prayer journey was to be in the spring of 1987 between Easter and Pentecost. It was to include seven European national capitols, located in both eastern and western Europe. A special team of prophetic ministries was to go together, along with a good number of intercessors, to support them.

"On this journey, we were to call the believers in every nation to reconciliation and unity. After humbling ourselves before the Lord and waiting upon Him, He promised to reveal to us the evil principalities in every nation, and we were to pull them down through prayer.

"In a final great proclamation meeting, we were to announce that the seventy years of Communism were coming to an end, and the power of this system was broken. We were to proclaim in every capitol city that that God was calling the Jews to return to Israel, and that the exodus from the North would begin. In the final display of praise, we were to release the spirit of evangelism detailed in Isaiah 61.

"God helped us to do this just as He commanded. It was the most amazing experience that I have ever had. God was carrying us on a wave of His Spirit and we knew that history was being made."

(THE FULL ARTICLE)

(Reprinted from *The Watchmen Ministry*)
Alpha and Omega Ministries, St. Louis, Missouri
By Rolland Smith

Because the crown is only for the conqueror (Rev. 3:21), the Church (later to become the Bride) must learn the art of spiritual warfare, of overcoming evil forces in preparation for her assumption of the throne following the Marriage Supper of the Lamb. To enable her to learn the technique of overcoming, God ordained the infinitely wise program of believer prayer. This world is a laboratory in which those destined for the throne are learning in actual practice how to overcome Satan and his hierarchy. The prayer closet is the arena which produces the overcomer." – Paul E. Billheimer

The army of God is actually two armies. One part is in heaven. The other part is on earth. Even though only on rare occasions have people been allowed to see the heavenly army, it does exist. In these last days, God is revealing His strategies concerning the cooperation of these two armies. Jacob saw these two armies in a vision. One of them was a mighty host of angels (the heavenly army), and the other was Jacob's family (the earthly army). To commemorate the vision, he named the place where the vision occurred – *Mahanaim*, which means "a double army." This place had great significance since it was the "re-entry point" of Jacob's return to Canaan, the border of the land of promise. It was here that Jacob sent word to his estranged brother, Esau, that he was coming home and desire to be reconciled with him.

David camped at this same location when his son, Absalom, rebelled and tried to take over the kingdom. Here again, there were two armies, but this time two armies of Israel were fighting each other. What a picture! The church must, in like manner, revisit *Mahanaim* if we are going to experience the uniting of the Body of Christ under the mighty Son of David, King Jesus, and if we are going to see the heavenly army take their position of protection over us, God's heritage.

The Lord Jesus chose to reveal this heavenly army to me in a most spectacular way. In March of 1984, I was in a time of deep prayer for several days. It started in a prayer conference in the northernmost part of Sweden, not far from the Arctic Circle. The theme of the prayer conference was "Preparing the Way of the Lord." A powerful prophetic anointing was on this conference and remained with me as I traveled toward southern Europe to Yugoslavia. At each stop along the way, the Lord Jesus met me in a most surprising way and led me into His glorious presence.

One of my stops was in Bro, Sweden, a small suburb of Stockholm. While I was there, two brothers and I were praying together in an apartment that was being renovated for Kjell and Lena Sjoberg. Kjell is a dear friend who is being used of God in a worldwide prophetic intercessory ministry.

As we interceded for Kjell's ministry and his home and office where he would spend so much time communicating with the Lord and with watchmen from around the world, a frightening thing happened to me. The presence of the Lord came so strong upon me that it pressed me down to the floor on my face. I was so overwhelmed by His glory that I could not look up or open my eyes. I became acutely aware that three angelic beings were standing in the room. There have been times before while worshipping God that I have felt His presence and even the presence of angels, but this time it was different. I was very conscious of their physical appearance and of their thoughts.

In spite of the overwhelming joy and peace flooding my whole being, it seemed very necessary to test these spirits, to see if they were truly sent by the Lord. Although there was a certainty forming in my heart that these glorious beings had been sent with important information, I wanted to be absolutely sure that they were not sent to deceive. Satan often comes as *an angel of light* with lying spirits, so according to I John 4:1-6, I challenged them to identify themselves. They began to praise the Lord Jesus Christ and declare His glory!

They shared many things with me. One told of all the battles they had fought side by side with the saints in other generations, including Joshua and David. As they spoke, my mind seemed to be instantly filled with understanding. I felt numb as the thought permeated my soul that I was in the presence of beings who had never died, but had lived throughout the entire history of the people of God.

The mind-boggling picture began to come into focus of how the armies of heaven are fighting alongside of God's sons and daughters here on earth. As I very timidly struggled to form a question that was forcing itself into my mind, I noticed a wariness on their faces similar to what I had seen on the faces of those who had spent long months on the front lines of major wars. They looked like battle-scarred veterans. I finally managed to whisper the nagging question, "Why haven't we won the war against the forces of Satan in the earth?" The answer they gave was embedded in my mind forever, "We have helped God's children to win the same territories many times, only to have them lost again to the Devil and his forces."

Their answer stung me to shame as my thoughts raced back over some of the dismal events in the history of the church, and the many glorious visitations of God's grace upon His people. Many times there have been dynamic expansions of the work of God among the nations, only to be followed by dark periods of coldness, hardness, rebellion, schisms, and devilish deceptions.

I could feel the quiet, steel-like strength of their never-ending vigilance and patience on the battlefield, as they stood motionless, waiting respectfully for my response. Their holy stillness and inner peace gave me strength to summon courage to speak one last time. It was a question that had risen up to torment my soul over and over all my life. It now came forcibly to my mind, "When will the war be over?" I asked hesitantly. As I posed this question, I was thinking of the promises in the Word of God when all the hordes of hell are finally vanquished, and all authorities and powers put under the feet of our Lord Jesus Christ, when His Kingdom will reign supreme over all the earth.

The answer came from the spokesman of the three, who had been standing just above my head, "The church on earth does not know or seem to care to understand what the invisible armies in heaven are doing. They are very preoccupied with their celebrations and feasts in my presence. When the church comprehends what we are doing and is ready to fight together with us in complete obedience to our glorious Head, Jesus Christ, then we will win the war."

Shortly after this, the brothers, who had been praying elsewhere in the apartment, came into the room where I was. They knew that something very powerful was happening. They did not see or hear anything but witnessed the strong presence of the Lord in the room. Although I tried, I failed in an attempt to share with them what I had seen and heard.

From there, I traveled to the west coast of Sweden where my wife, Carrie, and I lived at the time, and made preparations to continue on to Yugoslavia.

On this trip, the Lord instructed me, very emphatically, to take along a certain brother to continuously pray for me, while I was ministering in conferences. His name was Oke Samuelsson. Oke was sure the Lord wanted him to go, but he had no money for the trip. I boarded the train for Copenhagen, the first leg of the journey, without him. But as I arrived at a station where I changed trains, there was Oke. God had spoken to a businessman named Gunnar Olsson to buy his ticket.

When we arrived in Zagreb, Yugoslavia, we were met by another Swede, Tommy Nauman, and a Yugoslavian brother, Stojan Gajicki. We drove in Tommy's small yellow European car to Beograd for a series of meetings. We drove down the main highway that connects Europe with the Middle East via Yugoslavia. It is called the highway of death because of so many fatalities caused by accidents. The roadway was in terrible condition so we had to drive very slowly most of the way.

On our return from Beograd to Zagreb, we decided to take the smaller back roads to avoid this terrible highway and all the traffic. After several hours, we were completely lost. The roads became very small and filled with many farm animals, tractors, horse-drawn wagons, etc. This predicament caused us to believe that perhaps God had led us to this remote place to pray for all these villages. Because Communism heavily influenced this part of the country, these people had few opportunities to hear the Gospel.

The four of us began to pray and bless every house, even the animals. As we continued for a long time in prayer, we began to praise the Lord in a most reverent way. Soon the little car was filled with the presence of Jesus, and we completely forgot about where we were.

Suddenly, the Spirit of God came over me as I sat in the left rear seat. I began to pray in a language I did not understand and had never prayed in before. As I prayed, it seemed as if a curtain moved away, and the heavens opened up. There before me was an enormous host of angels. As far as the eye could see in all directions, the heavens were filled with angels. I lost all sense of where I was and seemed to be lifted up into the very presence of these angels. I could see in great detail.
There was much activity everywhere with singing, shouting, and a kaleidoscope of brilliant lights of every color flaring out into the heavens. Yet, in spite of all this flurry of motion, there was a strange sense of order. There was no confusion.

The Lord Jesus Christ was in the center of it all. It was almost a shock to see Him. So striking was His appearance that He dominated everything. The look on His face was so filled with expression it was as if I could see deep into His soul. I saw an expression of joy, yet it seemed to be mixed with deep, sorrowful compassion. I had an unmistakable feeling that He had waited for a very long time for this day to come, and now He was ready to act.

The air was filled with anticipation that something extraordinary was about to happen. I thought I was witnessing the throne room of God, yet Jesus was not on a throne. He stood at a large desk, similar to a bar of justice in a courtroom where the judge sits. Behind Him was a huge bookshelf lined with volumes of very large books. They were very old books, bound with thick leather covers, and securely locked. The Lord took one of these books, laid it on the desk, and unlocked it.

He then began to take the pages from the book, one at a time. As He took a page, a trumpet blast was sounded, and a band of mighty angels came forward and stood before the Lord in rapt attention. They were enormously powerful and beautiful beings. With great solemnity, the Lord Jesus Christ presented each band with a page from the book. The Lord spoke briefly to the group and commanded them to go quickly. Then, with a mighty flash of light, the angels flew away.

This process was repeated hundreds of times, with each band of angels being given a single page from the book, and sent forth by the Lord. This continued until every page was removed from the large book. Then, Jesus would turn and select another of the strange ancient chronicles, open it very carefully, and begin to give out each page to the summoned band of His faithful heavenly servants.

As I watched, I continued to utter the strange language. The thought went through my mind that the Holy Spirit was speaking out of my mouth the same words that were going out of the mouth of the Lord. I was transfixed. It seemed like I was not even breathing. Time must have stood still. What I was witnessing should have taken hours to complete.

Finally, one large section of what must have been hundreds of thousands, perhaps millions of angels, were all sent forth. It became clear that a whole army of angels had been dispatched by the Lord into different parts of the earth. I shuddered as a huge, awesome angel came forth and blew a loud, long blast on a golden trumpet. This caused millions of angels on two sides of the Lord to change their positions. There was a mighty shift, and about half of the angels who remained stood directly in front of the Lord Jesus. It was evident that this was a distinct army of angels, with recognizable leaders. They stood in perfect order, row upon row, reaching to the horizon.

The Lord of Hosts began to repeat just what He had done with the first army of angels. A large, thick book was opened, and with much gravity, the Lord would take a page and give it to a selected band of angels. They would be sent forth with very specific directions.

By some means, I seemed to be brought much closer to the scene immediately around the Lord Jesus. As this happened, I was able to actually look at the pages as they were handed out by the Lord. The paper was very old parchment. The loose-leaf volumes were thick, with richly carved leather-bound covers. It looked like it had been written a very long time ago.

As the pages became visible to me, I noticed that there were maps drawn on about half of the page, with handwritten notes filling the rest of the space. The maps obviously had a very special purpose.

They were geographical maps of a fairly large region, with rivers, mountains, roads, and other landmarks drawn on them. Also, there were symbols and arrows identifying various locations and directions. These drawings were like those in a war-room of a military headquarters where the commanding officers direct war operations.

Finally, this second vast army was commissioned to go forth with their written assignments until not one angel was left. Many of the large volumes had been emptied of their sealed documents, yet there were still more great books left.

There was now only one army left in heaven. It was the giant choir of angels that stood behind the Lord, in long arching lines, each row slightly higher than the one in front of it. It seemed there were not quite so many as in the two previous armies.

The environment seemed to change somewhat. The light was just as bright, the glory was everywhere, but millions of angels had left now, and their places were empty. The Lord continued to open the books, and He now signaled for the final remnant of the unnumbered hosts of heaven. He suddenly changed His orders somewhat.

Until now, I could not understand at all just what the angels had been sent forth to do. A strange sensation was beginning to dawn upon me. I felt, without really knowing, that the angels had been sent to do battle all over the world, but there was also a feeling of uncertainty about this assumption. But, as the Lord began to assign the remaining forces of angels, this time He spoke more in detail as He handed each band their proper page. He was sending them to the churches, and they were to give wisdom and assistance to the people of God so that they could learn to do warfare in worship. They were told to teach them the music of heaven, and release a new anointing in the worship that would cause great fear to come into the ranks of the enemies of God.

Finally, the very last angel was sent forth from the presence of the Lord. The only ones left were four extremely large creatures. They were much larger than I had previously seen, and they appeared to be on fire. Blazing fire and red-hot coals completely covered them. It was very difficult to focus my eyes on them. They moved constantly, looking in all directions as a bodyguard would, watching for any intruder. When they moved, there was a strange rumbling sound like deep thunder, or perhaps like great waterfalls thundering unceasingly. They surrounded the Lord Jesus Christ on all sides, protecting Him, yet showing the greatest reverence and awe of Him in their every move.

Just as suddenly as this vision began, it ended as I found myself back in the car. For several minutes I could not move. Then, as the surroundings became familiar again, I tried to speak, but I could not control my mouth. The feeling in my lips and tongue was similar to having received a shot of Novocaine.

It was obvious to everyone in the car that something very unusual had just occurred. They were all talking at once, trying to understand what had happened, but I could not speak for some time. Slowly the numbness in my mouth began to subside, but I was so deeply shaken by what I had seen I could not describe it to them. Nothing even remotely like this had ever happened to me before in my entire life. I spoke a few sentences, but was unsuccessful in explaining to them what I had seen.

Several hours later we finally arrived at Zagreb. Even then I could not eat, and later that night could hardly sleep. The urge to understand what I had seen was so strong that I decided to fast until the Lord gave me clear comprehension. I was sure that the next day, we would hear on the news that the third world war had begun. I was convinced that the angels must have been going into war. It did not seem that they were to wait one moment, but start executing their battle strategies that very instant.

The next day, Oke Samuelsson and I returned to Germany for two conferences in which I was scheduled to teach. The first conference was at the Youth with a Mission (YWAM) training center at Hurlach, Germany, a short distance outside Munich. During these training sessions I taught on spiritual warfare and intercession. However, I did not mention what I had experienced in Yugoslavia. Oke and I prayed all the time between sessions, on our faces in our room, crying out to God for the answers concerning the angelic visitation.

I left the YWAM base without any answers. We then went to the second conference, which was held at an old hotel high in the mountains, south of Munich, where Hitler had his mountain fortress, Eagle's Nest. It was a beautiful hotel that had been built for his most trusted officers to get away for rest.

This conference was for men and women in the United States military stationed in Europe. All who attended were deeply committed Christians who had come with their families to be spiritually refreshed. Many were high-ranking officers with very critical military responsibilities. Again, I spoke on spiritual warfare and intercession. This time I tried to share, very briefly, some of what I had seen. I could not bring myself to go into detail. It seemed to be so very sacred. I felt I could somehow corrupt it if I spoke of it too much or possibly any at all.

In the very last session, we were sharing communion around the Lord's Table. As we were breaking the bread, the Lord Jesus opened my understanding and spoke softly into my heart. He began to explain what I had seen in the vision in detail. He spoke with a voice, which expressed deep satisfaction and firmness. "What you saw," He said, "was not the angels going into battle alone. I was sending them to My servants all over the world. Today I have found faithful and trustworthy men and women all over the world. Just as the military must subject soldiers to very severe tests to verify their trustworthiness with the secrets of war, defenses, weaponry, and battle plans; so I have also subjected my servants to the most severe tests for faithfulness. Now, I have, for the first time in the history of the world such people positioned in every part of the entire globe."

My heartbeat rapidly, and I rejoiced as the Lord opened my understanding. He said, "The angels were sent to my trusted servants. I have ordered My angels to reveal My deep secrets; My battle plans for the final war to overthrow the forces of all my enemies. The heavenly army will be on assignment to fight together with them. They will teach them wisdom much as I sent them to teach Daniel wisdom while he was in captivity. These trusted servants will not reveal my plans to the enemy! They will obey me!"

Jesus continued to speak deep into my heart. "The maps you saw were the assignments to my servants. The angels were sent to deliver them. Every geographical area in the world is included. These are my officers ready to assume the command of my army throughout the earth. These are captains, called to raise up the army of God in their territory, and lead them into battle to take the region over which I have given them authority. There is much more, but I will tell you more when you need to know."

All during 1984 I waited for more from the Lord. Then, suddenly, on New Year's Eve of that year the Lord spoke again. Jesus said, "Those who were given these assignments will begin to develop strategies of prayer and evangelism for whole nations, multi-national regions, and whole continents. Networks will be formed among vast numbers of God's servants and will stretch out over the whole earth in mighty "outreaches." Even global strategies will be given."

All this was deeply moving down in my soul. I rejoiced. I hoped. I expected to see these things begin to happen at any moment. It never occurred to me that I might be one of those in the vision who would be called and entrusted by the Lord to take part in mobilizing this glorious army of God.

Even as He began to speak to me, in January of 1985, concerning a special prayer journey He wanted me to lead, I never connected it with the vision. I only knew that the Lord was moving in a very prophetic way to speak a message over the whole of Europe that would forever change that continent.

Jesus said that this prophetic prayer journey was to be in the spring of 1987 between Easter and Pentecost. It was to include seven European national capitols, located in both eastern and western Europe. A special team of prophetic ministries was to go together, along with a good number of intercessors, to support them.

On this journey, we were to call the believers in every nation to reconciliation and unity. After humbling ourselves before the Lord and waiting upon Him, He promised to reveal to us the evil principalities in every nation, and we were to pull them down through prayer.

In a final great proclamation meeting, we were to announce that the seventy years of Communism were coming to an end, and the power of this system was broken. We were to proclaim in every capitol city that that God was calling the Jews to return to Israel, and that the exodus from the North would begin. In the final display of praise, we were to release the spirit of evangelism detailed in Isaiah 61.

God helped us to do this just as He commanded. It was the most amazing experience that I have ever had. God was carrying us on a wave of His Spirit and we knew that history was being made.

IV. CONCLUSION

What Rolland Smith saw was true. We are the generation to whom these strategies are being given. We are the people, and this is the time. We are the church that is positioned to receive wisdom from God, so that we can do our part in His plan.

Come, Lord Jesus, come quickly, come! It's all about You. It's not about us and it's not even about Your angels. It's Your Kingdom that's coming, Lord. Fulfill Your promises. Execute Your end-time plans! We stand before You, as ready as we can be. Prepare us; make us part of Your army; keep us alert and responsive to You. We love you! Highest praises to You. Amen!

Reflection Questions
Lesson Twelve: Angels and God's End Time Army

Answers to these questions can be found in the back of the study guide.

Fill in the Blank

1. Angels will gather the _____ and the _____.

2. Psalm 149 declares that the _____ _____ of God are supernatural weapons of spiritual warfare.

Multiple Choice – Choose the best answer from the list below:

A.	Watchers	C.	Beings
B.	Strategies	D.	Miracles

3. Angels are divine _____.

4. God is releasing His _____ to our generation so we can do our part in His plan.

True or False

5. Angels have a limited number of tasks assigned to them. _____

6. Angelic praise can be heard by humans. _____

7. End-time events are not affected by our daily choices. _____

Continued on the next page.

Reflection and Journaling

8. Look back at the insights you wrote down in the previous lessons.

Journal concluding thoughts about what you have learned through this entire study and how you want to act differently as a result.

Pray using the revelation the Lord has given to you. Tell Him your desire to be a part of His end-time army.

Appendix One:
Scriptures about Angels

Genesis
Gen. 3:24
Gen. 16:7, 9-11
Gen. 19:1, 15
Gen. 21:17
Gen. 22:11, 15
Gen. 24:7, 40
Gen. 28:12
Gen. 31:11
Gen. 32:1
Gen. 48:16

Exodus
Exod. 3:2
Exod. 14:19
Exod. 23:20-23
Exod. 25:18-20, 22
Exod. 26:1, 31
Exod. 32:34
Exod. 33:2
Exod. 36:8, 35
Exod. 37:7-9

Numbers
Num. 7:89
Num. 20:16
Num. 22:22-27, 31-32, 35

Deuteronomy
Deut. 4:19
Deut. 17:3

Joshua
Josh. 5:14-15

Judges
Judg. 2:1, 4
Judg. 5:23
Judg. 6:11-12, 20-22
Judg. 13:3, 6, 9, 13-18, 20-21

I Samuel
I Sam. 4:4
I Sam. 16:14-23
I Sam. 18:10
I Sam. 19:9

II Samuel
II Sam. 6:2
II Sam. 22:11
II Sam. 24:16-17

I Kings
I Kings 6:23-29, 32, 35
I Kings 7:29, 36
I Kings 8:6-7
I Kings 19:5, 7
I Kings 22:19

II Kings
II Kings 1:3, 15
II Kings 17:16
II Kings 19:15, 35
II Kings 21:3, 5
II Kings 23:4-5

I Chronicles
I Chron. 13:6
I Chron. 21:1, 12, 15-16,
18,20,27,30
I Chron. 28:18

II Chronicles
II Chron. 3:7, 10-14
II Chron. 5:7-8
II Chron. 18:18
II Chron. 32:21
II Chron. 33:3, 5

Job
Job 1–2

Psalms
Ps. 18:10
Ps. 33:6
Ps. 34:7
Ps. 35:5-6
Ps. 78:49
Ps. 80:1
Ps. 91:11
Ps. 99:1
Ps. 103:20
Ps. 148:2

Isaiah
Isa. 4:4
Isa. 6:2, 6
Isa. 14:12
Isa. 34:4
Isa. 37:16, 36
Isa. 63:9

Jeremiah
Jer. 19:3
Jer. 33:22

Ezekiel
Ezek. 1:5-22
Ezek. 3:13
Ezek. 9:3
Ezek. 10:1-9, 14-20
Ezek. 11:22
Ezek. 28:14, 16
Ezek. 41:18, 20, 25

Daniel
Dan. 3:28
Dan. 4:13, 17, 23, 35
Dan. 6:22
Dan. 8:10-13, 16
Dan. 9:21
Dan. 10:13, 21
Dan. 12:1

Hosea
Hos. 12:4

Zephaniah
Zeph. 1:5

Zechariah
Zech. 1:9, 11-14, 19
Zech. 2:3
Zech. 3:1-6
Zech. 4:1, 4-5, 11
Zech. 5:5, 10
Zech. 6:4-5

Matthew
Matt. 1:20, 24
Matt. 2:13, 19
Matt. 4:1-11
Matt. 8–9
Matt. 12:26, 43-45
Matt. 13:39, 41, 49
Matt. 16:27
Matt. 17:18
Matt. 18:10
Matt. 22:30
Matt. 24:31, 36
Matt. 25:31, 41
Matt. 26:53
Matt. 28:2, 5

Mark
Mark 1:13, 23-26
Mark 3:23, 26
Mark 4:15
Mark 5
Mark 7:26-30
Mark 8:38
Mark 9:25-26
Mark 12:25
Mark 13:27, 32
Mark 16:5

Luke

Luke 1:11-13, 18-19, 26, 28, 30, 34-35, 38

Luke 2:9-10, 13, 15, 21

Luke 4:2-12, 33-36

Luke 8:12, 27-39

Luke 9:26, 42

Luke 10:18

Luke 11:14-18, 24-26

Luke 12:8-9

Luke 13:16

Luke 15:10

Luke 16:22

Luke 20:36

Luke 22:3, 31, 42

Luke 24:23

John

John 1:51

John 5:4

John 8:44

John 12:29

John 13:2, 27

John 20:12

Acts

Acts 1:10

Acts 5:3, 19

Acts 7:30, 35, 38

Acts 7:42, 53

Acts 8:26

Acts 10:3-4, 7, 22, 38

Acts 11:13

Acts 12:7-11, 15, 23

Acts 13:10

Acts 19:13-16

Acts 23:8-9

Acts 26:18

Acts 27:23

Romans

Rom. 8:38

Rom. 16:20

I Corinthians

I Cor. 5:5

I Cor. 10:10

I Cor. 4:9

I Cor. 6:3

I Cor. 7:5

I Cor. 11:10

I Cor. 13:1

II Corinthians

II Cor. 2:11

II Cor. 11:14

II Cor. 12:7

Galatians

Gal. 1:8

Gal. 3:19

Ephesians

Eph. 4:27

Eph. 6:11

Colossians

Col. 2:18

I Thessalonians

I Thess. 2:18

II Thessalonians

II Thess. 1:7

II Thess. 2:9

I Timothy

I Tim. 1:20

I Tim. 3:6-7, 16

I Tim. 5:15, 21

II Timothy

II Tim. 2:26

Hebrews

Heb. 1:4-7, 13

Heb. 2:2, 5,7,9,14,16

Heb. 9:5

Heb. 12:22

James
James 4:7

I Peter
I Pet. 1:12
I Pet. 3:22
I Pet. 5:8

II Peter
II Pet. 2:4, 10-11

I John
I John 3:8, 10
I John 4:3

Jude
Jude 1:6-9

Revelation
Rev. 1:1, 20
Rev. 2:1, 8-10, 12-13, 18, 24
Rev. 3:1, 5, 7,9,14
Rev. 4:6-9
Rev. 5:2, 6, 8, 11, 14
Rev. 6:1, 6
Rev. 7:1-2, 11
Rev. 8:2-8, 10, 12-13
Rev. 9:1, 11, 13-15
Rev. 10:1, 5, 7, 8-10
Rev. 11:15
Rev. 12:7, 9, 12
Rev. 14:3, 6, 8-10, 15, 17-19
Rev. 15:1, 6-8
Rev. 16:1-5, 8,10,12,17
Rev. 17:1, 3,7,15
Rev. 18:1, 21
Rev. 19:4, 9, 17
Rev. 20:1-2, 7, 10
Rev. 21:9, 12, 15, 17
Rev. 22:6, 8, 16

Answers to the Reflection Questions

Lesson One – Jacob's Ladder Keeps Coming Down
1. before, again
2. spirits, designs
3. past, current; nations
4. A
5. C
6. False   7. True   8. True

Lesson Two – My Personal Angelic Encounters
1. "flavors"
2. False   3. True

Lesson Three – Invaded!
1. Fear not
2. relationship, cling
3. disciple
4. B
5. C
6. True   7. False

Lesson Four – The Nature of These Celestial Beings
1. messenger
2. deputies, righteousness
3. Michael, Gabriel, Raphael, Uriel, Lucifer
4. D
5. B
6. True   7. True   8. True

Lesson Five – The Characteristics of Angels
1. Jesus Christ (before His incarnation)
2. cherubs (angels)
3. sons of God, ministering spirits, heavenly host, God's holy ones, watchers
4. A
5. C
6. True   7. False   8. True

Lesson Six – Angelic Assignments
1. service to God, service to Christians, perform God's Word
2. Michael, intercession
3. C
4. B
5. True   6. True

Lesson Seven – Jesus and the Ministering Angels
1. preincarnate
2. early infancy, wilderness, Gethsemane, crucifixion
3. A
4. D
5. True   6. True

Lesson Nine – Discerning the Angelic Presence

1. source, operation
2. Do not worship, Do not revile, Judge messages
3. people, God
4. hear, see, feel, in dreams, in visions
5. True   6. False

Lesson Ten – Angelic Intervention through Intercession

1. intercession
2. individuals, nations
3. up, down
4. C
5. D
6. False   7. True   8. True

Lesson Eleven – Israel, the Harvest and the End Times

1. Angels, Israel
2. "grafted in"
3. Egypt, Syria, inexplicably
4. B
5. D
6. True   7. False   8. True

Lesson Twelve – Angels and God's End Time Army

1. lawless, elect
2. high praises
3. A
4. B
5. False   6. True   7. False

Resource Materials

H.A. Baker, *Visions Beyond the Veil,* Tonbridge, England: Sovereign World, 2000.

Margaret Barker, *An Extraordinary Gathering of Angels,* London: MQ Publications, 2004.

Book of Enoch online by going to
http://www.heaven.net.nz/writings/thebookofenoch.htm.

From "The Key of Breakthrough," by Shawn Bolz, as published on The Elijah List, July 3, 2006, www.elijahlist.com/words/display_word/4248. Accessed Nov. 20, 2006. Used with permission.

Roland Buck, *Angels on Assignment* , New Kensington, PA: Whitaker House, 1979).

John Calvin, *Institutes,* [numerous editions], Book First, Chapter 14, excerpted from Sections 5, 6, and 9.

Paul Keith Davis in the E-Newsletter of White Dove Ministries dated 11/2005, (http://www.whitedoveministries.org/content/NewsItem.phtml?art=292&c=0&id=30&style

Paul Keith Davis, "Breakthrough Revival," as posted on The Elijah List, April 4, 2006, www.elijahlist.com/words/display_word/3959. Accessed Nov. 7, 2006. Used with permission.

Excerpted from Geoffrey Dennis (Rabbi), "Angels," *Encyclopedia Mythica Online* (http://www.pantheon.org/articles/a/angels.html), copyright 2004 Geoffrey Dennis. (Accessed September 29, 2006).

James W. Goll, *Exodus Cry,* Ventura, CA: Regal Books, 2001).

James W. Goll, *Kneeling on the Promises* (Grand Rapids, Mich.: Baker/Chosen Books, 1999).

James W. Goll, *The Seer: The Prophetic Power of Visions, Dreams, and Open Heavens*, Shippensburg, PA: Destiny Image Publishers, Inc., 2004).

Billy Graham, *Angels,* Nashville, TN: Thomas Nelson/W Publishing Group, 1995), p. 30.

Matthew Henry's Commentary on the Whole Bible: New Modern Edition, Electronic Database, Peabody, MA: Hendrickson Publishers, Inc., 1991), excerpted from commentary on Genesis 28.

From Lance Lambert, *Battle for Israel,* Eastbourne, East Sussex, England: Kingsway Publications, 1975.

Martin Luther, *Table Talk* [numerous editions], excerpted from Section DLXV, "Of Angels."

Pascal P. Parente, *Beyond Space,* Rockford, IL: Tan Books and Publishers, 1973), 18-19. Quote from St. Augustine comes from his Sermon on Psalm 103, I, 15.

Roland Smith, *The Watchmen Ministry Manual,* Alpha and Omega Ministries, St. Louis, MO: Reprinted with permission.

The Catholic Encyclopedia, online edition, "Angels," citing Gregory's Homily #34, in *Evangelium* ("Gospel," Breviary) (http://www.newadvent.org/cathen/01476d.htm). Accessed November 27, 2006.

Bill Yount, "Something Sweeter Than Chocolate Is Now Coming Forth Out of Hershey, Pennsylvania," as published on The Elijah List, November 18, 2005, www.elijahlist.com. Accessed August 10, 2006.

End Notes

1   *Matthew Henry's Commentary on the Whole Bible: New Modern Edition,* Electronic Database (Peabody, Mass.: Hendrickson Publishers, Inc., 1991), excerpted from commentary on Genesis 28. Italics mine.

2   H.A. Baker, *Visions Beyond the Veil* (Tonbridge, England: Sovereign World, 2000), p. 40.

3   Ibid., pp. 42-43.

4   Retold from Chapter 3 of my book, *Kneeling on the Promises* (Grand Rapids, Mich.: Baker/Chosen Books, 1999), 65-66, and from another book of mine, *Exodus Cry* (Ventura, Calif.: Regal Books, 2001), 166-67.

5   Martin Luther, *Table Talk* [numerous editions], excerpted from Section DLXV, "Of Angels."

6   John Calvin, *Institutes,* [numerous editions], Book First, Chapter 14, excerpted from Sections 5, 6, and 9.

7   Margaret Barker, *An Extraordinary Gathering of Angels* (London: MQ Publications, 2004), 10.

8   Pascal P. Parente, *Beyond Space* (Rockford, Ill.: Tan Books and Publishers, 1973), 18-19. Quote from St. Augustine comes from his Sermon on Psalm 103, I, 15.

9   Excerpted from Geoffrey Dennis (Rabbi), "Angels," *Encyclopedia Mythica Online* (http://www.pantheon.org/articles/a/angels.html), copyright 2004 Geoffrey Dennis. (Accessed September 29, 2006).

10   Billy Graham, *Angels,* Nashville, TN: Thomas Nelson/W Publishing Group, 1995), p. 30.

11   According to the Catholic Encyclopedia (Ibid.), "the only Scriptural names furnished of individual angels are Raphael, Michael, and Gabriel, names which signify their respective attributes. Apocryphal Jewish books, such as the Book of Enoch [and Esdras], supply those of Uriel and Jeremiel, while many are found in other apocryphal sources, like those Milton names in 'Paradise Lost.'"

12   You can read the Book of Enoch online by going to http://www.heaven.net.nz/writings/thebookofenoch.htm.

13   The Catholic Encyclopedia, online edition, "Angels," citing Gregory's Homily #34, in *Evangelium* ("Gospel," Breviary) (http://www.newadvent.org/cathen/01476d.htm). Accessed November 27, 2006.

14   See story by Paul Keith Davis in the E-Newsletter of WhiteDove Ministries, 11/2005, (http://www.whitedoveministries.org/content/NewsItem.phtml?art=292&c=0&id=30&style=), accessed December 8, 2006.

15   Ibid., Paul Keith Davis.

16   Op. cit., Billy Graham, pp. 139-41.

17   Op. cit., Billy Graham, pp. 156-57.

[18] From "Something Sweeter Than Chocolate Is Now Coming Forth Out of Hershey, Pennsylvania," by Bill Yount, as published on The Elijah List, November 18, 2005, www.elijahlist.com. Accessed August 10, 2006. Used with permission.

[19] Roland Buck, *Angels on Assignment* (New Kensington, Penna.: Whitaker House, 1979).

[20] James W. Goll, *The Seer: The Prophetic Power of Visions, Dreams, and Open Heavens* (Shippensburg, PA: Destiny Image Publishers, Inc., 2004).

[21] From Lance Lambert, *Battle for Israel* (Eastbourne, East Sussex, England: Kingsway Publications, 1975), 9, 11-13.

[22] Ibid., 13,14.

[23] Ibid., 17-18.

[24] Ibid., 111.

[25] Paul Keith Davis, "Breakthrough Revival," as posted on The Elijah List, April 4, 2006, www.elijahlist.com/words/display_word/3959. Accessed Nov. 7, 2006. Used with permission.

[26] From "The Key of Breakthrough," by Shawn Bolz, as published on The Elijah List, July 3, 2006, www.elijahlist.com/words/display_word/4248. Accessed Nov. 20, 2006. Used with permission.

[27] Roland Smith, "The Watchman Ministry Manual", Alpha and Omega Ministries, St. Louis, MO, Reprinted by permission.

About the Author

James W. Goll is a lover of Jesus who co-founded Encounters Network (based in Franklin, Tennessee), which is dedicated to changing lives and impacting nations by releasing God's presence through prophetic, intercessory and compassion ministry. James is the International Director of Prayer Storm, a 24/7/365 prayer media-based ministry. He is also the Founder of the God Encounters Training E-School of the Heart – where faith and life meet.

After pastoring in the Midwest, James was thrust into the role of itinerant teaching and training around the globe. He has traveled extensively to every continent, carrying a passion for Jesus wherever he goes. James desires to see the Body of Christ become the house of prayer for all nations and be empowered by the Holy Spirit to spread the Good News around the world. He is the author of numerous books and training manuals as well as a contributing writer for several periodicals.

He is a member of the Harvest International Ministry Apostolic Team and a consultant to several national and international ministries. James and Michal Ann Goll were married for more than 32 years before her graduation to heaven in the fall of 2008. They have four wonderful adult married children, and James continues to make his home in greater Nashville, Tennessee.

Other Books by James W. and Michal Ann Goll

God Encounters

Prayer Storm

Intercession

A Radical Faith

Women on the Frontlines Series

The Lost Art of Intercession

The Lost Art of Practicing His Presence

The Lost Art of Pure Worship

The Coming Israel Awakening

The Beginner's Guide to Hearing God

The Coming Prophetic Revolution

The Call of the Elijah Revolution

The Prophetic Intercessor

The Seer Expanded

The Seer Devotional and Journal

James W. Goll 365 Day Personal Prayer Guide

Shifting Shadows of Supernatural Experiences

The Lifestyle of a Prophet

Empowered Prayer

Empowered Women

Dream Language

Angelic Encounters

Adventures in the Prophetic

Praying for Israel's Destiny

Living a Supernatural Life

Deliverance from Darkness

Exploring Your Dreams and Visions

God's Supernatural Power in You

The Reformer's Pledge

Prayer Changes Things

In addition there are numerous study guides including Discovering the Seer in You, Exploring the Gift and Nature of Dreams, Prayer Storm, A Radical Faith, Deliverance from Darkness, Prophetic Foundations, Walking in the Supernatural Life, Consecrated Contemplative Prayer and many others with corresponding CD and MP3 albums and DVD messages.

For More Information:

James W. Goll
Encounters Network
P.O. Box 1653
Franklin, TN 37065
Visit: www.encountersnetwork.com
www.prayerstorm.com
www.GETeSchool.com

Email: info@encountersnetwork.com
Speaking Invitations: inviteEN@gmail.com

Resources

Encounters Network
changing lives ❖ impacting nations

P.O. Box 1653 | Franklin, TN 37065-1653
www.encountersnetwork.com | 1.877.200.1604

COMPASSION ACTS
love taking action

Love Taking Action

♦ Mission Projects
sending resources and volunteers to help meet specific needs

♦ Rice Shipments
shipping fortified rice to fight hunger around the world

♦ Emergency Relief
responding to natural disasters through food and humanitarian aid

♦ Project Dreamers Park
building playgrounds and community centers to inspire children to dream

♦ First Nations in America
serving Native Americans by providing food, health supplies and education

Compassion Acts is a network of synergistic relationships between people, ministries and organizations, focused on bringing hope for our day through the power of compassion and prayer. We desire to demonstrate love and encourage the hearts of those impacted by poverty, disease, political strife and natural disasters through human relief efforts.

www.compassionacts.com

PRAYERSTORM

The Hour that Changes the World

Leviticus 6:13
"Fire must be kept burning on the altar continually; it must not got out."

Worldwide 24/7
Hourly Intercession Targeting:

♦ Revival in the Church

♦ Prayer for Israel

♦ World's Greatest Youth Awakening

♦ Crisis Intervention through Intercession

The vision of **PrayerStorm** is to restore and release the Moravian model of the watch of the Lord into churches, homes and prayer rooms around the world. Web-based teaching, prayer bulletins and resources are utilized to facilitate round-the-clock worship and prayer to win for the Lamb the rewards of His suffering.

Releasing the Global Moravian Lampstand

www.prayerstorm.com

Encounters Network
changing lives ✣ impacting nations

Changing Lives ✣ Impacting Nations

♦ Empowering Believers
through training and resources

♦ EN Media
relevant messages for our day

♦ God Encounters Training
e-school of the heart

♦ EN Alliance
a coalition of leaders

The vision of **Encounters Network** is to unite and mobilize the body of Christ by teaching and imparting the power of intercession and prophetic ministry, while cultivating God's heart for Israel. We accomplish this through networking with leaders in the church and marketplace; equipping believers through conferences and classes, utilizing various forms of relevant media; and creating quality materials to reproduce life in the Spirit.

www.encountersnetwork.com

Introduction to God Encounters Training School

If you are seeking to grow in your intimacy with God and mature in your walk of faith, if you desire to cultivate the spirit of revelation and live a life of power in the Spirit, then begin your journey by joining God Encounters Training – eSchool of the Heart.

Biblically-based study materials in both physical and electronic formats, combined with Spirit-led teaching, are now yours to experience on a personal level. These correspondence courses may be taken for credit towards graduation from the God Encounters Training School.

What Others Are Saying:

Goll's extraordinary ability to think through crucial issues and his skill at expressing the solutions in terms that the average believer can understand, comes through loud and clear in his materials.

~ **C. Peter Wagner**, noted author, professor, President of Global Harvest Ministries, Chancellor Emeritus of the Wagner Leadership Institute

The Lord has given James Goll insights into Scripture as it relates to the foundation of each believer and vision for the Body of Christ. His curriculum will powerfully strengthen the spiritual life of any person, group, or congregation that will use them.

~ **Don Finto**, author, pastor emeritus of Belmont Church in Nashville, TN and director of the Caleb Company

 For Course Information and Registration Visit
www.GETeSchool.com

GET eSchool Courses & Corresponding Study Guides

CHAMBER OF ACTION
EXPLORING PRINCIPLES - EXPERIENCING POWER

DELIVERANCE FROM DARKNESS

You shall know the truth and the truth shall set you free! Through this accessible and easy-to-use guide, you will learn how to: recognize demonic entities and their strategies, equip yourself to overcome the demonic, keep yourself refreshed during the fight, bring healing through blessing, and much more!

THE HEALING ANOINTING

In this thorough study guide, James W. Goll covers a range of topics including: The Healing Ministry of Jesus, How to Move In and Cooperate with the Anointing, Healing the Wounded Spirit, Overcoming Rejection, the Five Stage Healing Model, and much more.

RELEASING SPIRITUAL GIFTS

In this study guide, James draws from scripture and adds perspective from many diverse streams to bring you clear definitions and exhort you into activation and release. The topics covered are subjects like: How Does the Holy Spirit Move, What Offends the Holy Spirit, and many other lessons from years of experience.

REVIVAL BREAKTHROUGH

James W. Goll brings 12 solid teachings on topics like: Prophetic Prayers for Revival, Classic Characteristics of Revival, Fasting Releases God's Presence, Creating an Opening, Gatekeepers of His Presence, and much more. This manual will inspire you to believe for a breakthrough in your life, neighborhood, region, city and nation for Jesus' sake!

WAR IN THE HEAVENLIES

These carefully prepared 12 detailed lessons on spiritual warfare cover topics like: The Fall of Lucifer, Dealing with Territorial Spirits, The Weapons of Our Warfare, High Praises, The Blood Sprinkled Seven Times, and other great messages. This is one of James' most thorough and complete manuals.

CHAMBER OF LIFE
BUILDING OUR FOUNDATION - KNOWING TRUTHS, GROWING IN FAITH

A RADICAL FAITH

Whether you are a veteran spiritual warrior or new believer, this accessible, comprehensive guide lays out the enduring biblical fundamentals that establish the bedrock of belief for every mature Christian. This handbook will help you build an indestructible foundation of radical faith.

DISCOVERING THE NATURE OF GOD

These lessons focus on the knowledge of God Himself. Lessons include: Laying a Proper Foundation, The Authority of God's Word, The Effects of God's Word, God as Our Father, The Nature of God, The Attributes of God, Jesus the Messiah, and more. Learn the nature of God and thus be transformed into His image.

WALKING IN THE SUPERNATURAL LIFE

James W. Goll weds together a depth of the Word with a flow of the Spirit that will ground and challenge you to live in the fullness for which God has created you. Topics include The God Who Never Changes, Tools for the Tool Belt, Finishing Well, and much more.

TO PURCHASE THESE STUDY GUIDES INDIVIDUALLY
& OTHER RELATED PRODUCT VISIT: WWW.ENCOUNTERSNETWORK.COM

For Course Information and Registration Visit
www.GETeSchool.com

GET eSchool Courses & Corresponding Study Guides

CHAMBER OF INTIMACY
BLUEPRINTS FOR PRAYER - PRELUDE TO REVIVAL

WATCHMEN ON THE WALLS

This original study guide is a classic in today's global prayer movement and covers many important and foundational lessons on intercession including: Fire on the Altar, Christ Our Priestly Model, The Watch of the Lord, From Prayer to His Presence, Identification in Intercession, and more.

COMPASSIONATE PROPHETIC INTERCESSION

These 12 lessons feature James W. Goll's finest teaching on the fundamentals of prophetic intercession and represent one of the primary messages of his life. Topics include Travail, Tears in the Bottle, Prophetic Intercession, The Power of Proclamation, Praying in the Spirit, and much more.

PRAYER STORM

This study guide sounds a worldwide call to consistent, persistent prayer for: revival in the church, the greatest youth awakening ever, Israel – and for all the descendents of Abraham, and God's intervention in times of major crises. Prayer Storm is an invitation into an international virtual house of prayer full of intercessors who commit to pray one hour per week.

PRAYERS OF THE NEW TESTAMENT

In this study guide, James goes through each of the scriptural prayers of the early church apostles and brings you a brief historical background sketch along with insights from the Holy Spirit for today. Learn what true apostolic intercession is, how to intercede with revelation, and how to cultivate a heart for your city and nation.

STRATEGIES OF INTERCESSION

In these 12 lessons, James W. Goll deals with issues like Confessing Generational Sins, Reminding God of His Word, Praying for Those in Authority, Praying on Site with Insight, and Praying Your Family into God's Family. It is a thorough and precise exposure to the many different strategies and models of prayer.

CONSECRATED CONTEMPLATIVE PRAYER

These 12 lessons have helped hundreds come into a deeper communion with their heavenly Father. James W. Goll brings understanding from the truths of Christian mystics of the past and builds on it with lessons from his own walk with the Lord. Topics include The Ministry of Fasting, Contemplative Prayer, Quieting Our Souls before God, and much more.

TO PURCHASE THESE STUDY GUIDES INDIVIDUALLY & OTHER RELATED PRODUCT VISIT: WWW.ENCOUNTERSNETWORK.COM

For Course Information and Registration Visit
www.GETeSchool.com

GET eSchool Courses & Corresponding Study Guides

 ## CHAMBER OF REVELATION
EQUIPPING IN THE PROPHETIC - ENLISTING A PROPHETIC ARMY

PROPHETIC FOUNDATIONS

Does God really speak to us personally today? If I listen, will I understand what He says? For those desiring to hear God, this course will show how anyone can both listen and speak to God. Lessons include: A Biblical History of the Prophetic, Intimacy in the Prophetic, Seven Expressions of the Prophetic, The Prophetic Song of the Lord, Responding to Revelation, and more.

MATURING IN THE PROPHETIC

You can grow in the things of the prophetic! These 12 lessons include: The Calling, Training and Commissioning; The Cross: The Prophetic Lifestyle; Pits and Pinnacles of the Prophetic; The Seer and the Prophet; Women in the Prophetic; and more. Character issues and relational dynamics are discussed at length.

RECEIVING AND DISCERNING REVELATION

This study guide will introduce you to the ways of God and the Spirit of Revelation and how to discern what is from the Holy Spirit and what is not. Learn to grow in your capacity to receive revelatory things from the Holy Spirit, and discern the voice and ways of God with nine scriptural tests to judging revelation.

THE SEER

What is the difference between a Seer and a Prophet? How do you cultivate the revelatory presence of the Lord? Is there a key that authentically opens the heavens? This guide helps you find and release the special gifts God has given to you, reveals how you can cultivate this realm of the prophetic in your life, and grounds you in the Word of God concerning prophetic gifts, dreams, visions, and open heavens.

DREAM LANGUAGE

This insightful study guide equips you for a greater understanding of the language of dreams, and grounds you in the Word of God concerning dreams and how to interpret them. This key to unlocking your gift of dreams explores: Cultivating a Culture for Revelation, Dream Drainers, Dream Busters, Why God Seems Silent and How to Cultivate the Realm of the Prophetic in your life.

UNDERSTANDING SUPERNATURAL ENCOUNTERS

This in-depth study guide contains 12 lessons that will give you insight on subjects like: Prophetic Gestures and Actions, Keys to the Supernatural, The Deception of the Anointing, Trances, Levels of Supernatural Visions, Order and Characteristics of Angels, Ministry and Function of Angels, and much more!

ANGELIC ENCOUNTERS TODAY

James and Michal Ann Goll use Scripture, church history, testimonies, and personal experience to: describe the different categories of angels, explain angels' ministry as God's agents to the world, demonstrate how intercession and angelic ministry are related, and show you how to perceive and engage angels in your own life.

  ## For Course Information and Registration Visit
www.GETeSchool.com

45136937R00092